FATHERHOOD

The Essential Guide

Tim
Atkinson

Fatherhood – The Essential Guide is also available in accessible formats for people with any degree of visual impairment. The large print edition and eBook (with accessibility features enabled) are available from Need2Know. Please let us know if there are any special features you require and we will do our best to accommodate your needs.

First published in Great Britain in 2011 by
Need2Know
Remus House
Coltsfoot Drive
Peterborough
PE2 9BF
Telephone 01733 898103
Fax 01733 313524
www.need2knowbooks.co.uk

Contents

Introduction

Becoming a father is one of the most important, exciting, absorbing and life-changing events in a man's life. There is nothing like it, and nothing that can fully prepare you for it. But 'forewarned is forearmed', as they say, and this book will help you discover what you need to know from the point of view of someone sometimes overlooked in other parenting guides and childcare manuals – you!

Although most dads today are present at the birth of their children and are happy to change nappies and generally pull their weight around the home, there's still a tendency to assume that it's just the mums who need to know precisely what to do. That's why most childcare books are addressed to mums, and dads might get a chapter somewhere if they're lucky.

This book is written by a dad for other dads. In the following pages you'll find structured guidance and up-to-date information reassuring you at every stage of the parenting process. The chapters start from the first idea of starting a family, through pregnancy and birth, right up to the first three years of your child's life. The book will answer your questions about what is happening to you, your partner and your baby and reassure you at each stage about what you need to do.

Chapter One

Planning a Family

Planning a family is a serious step in anyone's life. Having children won't be like anything else you'll have ever done. No matter how well prepared you think you are, there will be plenty of surprises in store. That's what makes children so exciting. And that's what makes the sleepless nights and dirty nappies worth enduring. As with everything else though, a little planning goes a long way. Accidents will happen, but having a child is such a life-changing experience that a little preparation can make all the difference. And that process starts long before you've bought your first pair of baby bootees!

Stopping contraception

For most people, the first step in planning to have children will be stopping contraception. Many people in long-term relationships use an oral contraceptive of some form. The pill is one of the most commonly used examples. Others, for various reasons, might use an IUD (intrauterine device) or 'coil'. Or your partner might be using contraceptive implants or injections. Clearly the first step on the road to having a baby is going to be deciding when to stop using contraception and, following that, when it will be safe to have unprotected sex. The two things may not happen simultaneously. Removing an IUD, for example, is something which has to be done by a GP or at the Family Planning Clinic, who may advise you to continue using condoms for a short while before trying for a baby. Contraceptive implants will also need to be removed under medical supervision, and continuing to use a condom is often recommended for at least a month when a woman stops using the pill in order to allow her menstrual cycle to return to normal.

'Planning a family is a serious step in anyone's life. Having children won't be like anything else you'll have ever done.'

The pill

Chemical contraceptives like the pill, along with implants and injections, stop fertility in a variety of ways. Most will prevent the ovum (egg) from ripening (ovulation) but some slow the progress of the egg or sperm, while others change the lining of the womb (endometrium) making it difficult for a fertilised egg to implant and start to grow. Obviously, it might take a little time for a woman's body to adjust after using the pill, and you need to bear this in mind when planning on starting a family.

Coming off the pill

'Advice is generally to stop smoking completely, and limit alcohol consumption to one or two units per week.'

Whatever form of pill your partner may be using, the advice is to allow at least one 'normal' monthly cycle before trying to get pregnant. This is so that when pregnancy does occur, it can be dated accurately. For this reason you may wish to use a condom for about a month after stopping the pill. Even if you've been using condoms regularly, you will both need to prepare for a healthy pregnancy. This is where the next section comes in.

Healthy eating and drinking

It goes without saying that eating and drinking healthily is going to make pregnancy and childbirth safer, as well as easier to cope with. Most people are aware of the health risks to the unborn child associated with smoking and alcohol consumption by women. Advice is generally to stop smoking completely, and limit alcohol consumption to one or two units per week. You might think that this doesn't affect dads much, if at all. But if you're a smoker, it means changes on your part too. Passive smoking will not only affect your partner, but can harm your unborn child as well. And excessive alcohol consumption can affect both the quantity and quality of your sperm, as well as making it more difficult to achieve and sustain an erection. You have been warned!

Smoking and drinking

Passive smoking is a real threat. There are hundreds of chemicals in tobacco smoke which are seriously harmful to the development of unborn children. Your partner and your unborn child will benefit from a healthy, smoke-free environment for the entire nine months of the pregnancy. And if you're having trouble conceiving, smoking and excessive drinking could well be part of the problem. Eliminating tobacco and cutting down your alcohol intake could immediately improve your chances of becoming a parent. Reduced sperm count, abnormal and unhealthy sperm and impotence are just some of the problems associated with excessive alcohol consumption in men. Stay within the government's safe limits (21 units per week for a man) or avoid alcohol completely while trying for a baby.

Food for fertility

Your partner will probably want to think about her eating and drinking long before becoming pregnant. And if you are both fans of high-fat, high-sugar items like cakes and biscuits, fizzy drinks and fast food, it'll be worth trying to cut them down or cut them out completely. Remember, you're in this together: where she goes, you should try to follow. It'll be encouragement for her and make you both feel better. And you'll need to be at the top of your game for what's to come.

Being overweight can also lead to serious problems during pregnancy. Pregnant women who are clinically obese are at risk of developing potentially dangerous pregnancy conditions such as pre-eclampsia, and the agency responsible for issuing health advice – the National Institute for Health and Clinical Excellence (NICE) – issued guidance recently (July 2010) encouraging women who are planning to get pregnant to attain a healthy weight before they start.

The UK Food Standards Agency (FSA) recommends that women trying to conceive or who are actually pregnant follow a diet containing:

▦ Five portions of fruit and vegetables per day. These can be fresh, frozen, tinned or dried; even a glass of juice qualifies.

▦ Carbohydrates, such as bread, pasta, rice (preferably wholegrain) and potatoes.

- Protein from such things as lean meat and chicken, fish, eggs and pulses (beans and lentils).

- Fish, including fresh tuna (not tinned, which doesn't count), mackerel, sardines and trout. Although oily fish is good, the FSA advises against having more than two portions per week.

- Dairy foods like milk, cheese and yoghurt, all of which contain calcium.

- Foods rich in iron, such as red meat, pulses, dried fruit, bread, green vegetables and fortified breakfast cereals. And it helps your body to absorb iron if you have some food or a drink containing vitamin C first.

Taking supplements

Although, for the most part, a healthy, balanced diet will give your partner enough vitamins and minerals to ensure she's in tip-top physical condition, some supplements are also recommended. Taking folic acid, for example, for at least six months before getting pregnant (as well as during the first 12 weeks of pregnancy) can dramatically reduce the chances of the baby having a number of birth defects, including spina bifida (a deformity of the spine).

Conception problems (and possible solutions)

Many things can affect your chances of conceiving. Some people are able to move from the decision to start a family, stopping contraception, straight to conception in one easy step. For other people there will be problems. It can take time. As the weeks and months go by, it can become stressful. There may be underlying health problems which need to be investigated and this can lead to long and sometimes painful medical tests. But many of the problems that traditionally meant couples couldn't conceive can now be remedied. The range of techniques available to assist or, in some cases, artificially achieve pregnancy has increased both in scope and reliability, and some of the most common procedures are discussed in the next section.

IVF and assisted pregnancy

In-vitro fertilisation, or IVF (literally, fertilisation 'in glass' – which in reality means on a Petri dish) is now the most common form of assistance given to couples struggling to conceive naturally. In some parts of the UK it is available free – or at least, subsidised – on the NHS. But if you do find yourself having to pay for a cycle, it can be costly and some clinics now offer couples a chance to take part in a donor-egg programme to offset the otherwise high fees.

How it works

IVF typically begins with a series of routine medical checks to make sure there are no underlying health problems, plus tests on the mobility and quality of the man's sperm. Once these have been completed, the woman begins a programme of hormone treatment designed to stimulate the growth of ovarian follicles and thus induce ovulation. Once the follicles are mature, the woman is injected with human chorionic gonadotropin (hCG) before the eggs are 'harvested'. This happens approximately 36 hours later.

Once the eggs (ova) have been harvested they are mixed with a sample of the man's sperm (donated in time-honoured fashion!) and left to fertilise. It's not uncommon for several of the eggs to develop into embryos, and due to the high number of multiple-births which used to be associated with IVF programmes, most clinics will now limit the number of these embryos re-implanted (into your partner's body) to just two or three. Once the healthiest embryos have been selected, they are placed back into the woman's fallopian tubes using a laparoscope.

Success rates

The success rate of IVF pregnancies varies greatly. A lot depends on the age of the couple, but other factors can affect the chance of fertilised embryos 'taking' when re-implanted. The biggest of these is the presence of chromosomal abnormalities in the developing foetus, but until recently there was no way of telling which, if any, of the embryos might be affected. Now, a new screening test for foetal abnormalities promises to double or even triple the chances of IVF success. It's thought that as many as 70% of miscarriages occur because of abnormalities in the foetal chromosomes, so screening the embryos before implanting them should greatly increase their viability.

What happens next?

If there has been no previous history of pregnancy complications then provided one or more of the re-implanted embryos 'takes' and the pregnancy is confirmed, your partner will be treated in the same way as if she'd got pregnant naturally. Occasionally hospitals do have special policies in place for dealing with IVF pregnancies but there is no reason to think that, once pregnant, your partner is any less likely to carry a baby to term than any other person.

Other fertility treatments

Occasionally, a man's sperm count is too low, or the sperm are too deformed, for fertilisation to take place 'semi-naturally' in the laboratory Petri dish. If this is the case, a further technique can be added to the above procedure. This involves physically injecting a single sperm into the egg, and is known as Intra-Cytoplasmic Sperm Injection, or ICSI.

Gamete intrafallopian transfer (GIFT) is another technique which follows the same procedures as IVF, except that fertilisation occurs inside the woman's body, as it would do normally. This is a slightly more invasive procedure, as the eggs are removed from the ovaries but placed in the fallopian tubes with a sample of the partner's sperm for fertilisation to take place.

Occasionally, problems with fertility are traced to the fact that there is no sperm present when a man ejaculates. This might mean abandoning all hope of conceiving, but it's possible that the man's testes will still be producing sperm. If this is the case, a technique called microsurgical epididymal sperm aspiration (MESA) or testicular sperm extraction (TESE) can be used to remove the sperm and fertilise the eggs in one of the above ways. For more information take a look at *Fertility – The Essential Guide* (Need2Know).

Pregnancy Tests

The chances of getting a false-positive result to a pregnancy test are so slight they are dismissed out of hand by most medics; the chances of a false-negative, however, are real – which is one reason why you often get two tests per pack. Once the little blue line appears, you know you're in this for real but there's still a long way to go. Some estimates suggest that up to 40% of pregnancies naturally terminate before the 12th week, often without the woman being aware that she's even been pregnant. That might seem difficult to believe (how could she not know?) but some women don't have a regular cycle, and their periods can vary in flow enormously. What might seem like a delayed or particularly heavy period might in fact be an early-term miscarriage.

'The chances of getting a false-positive result to a pregnancy test are so slight they are dismissed out of hand by most medics; the chances of a false-negative, however, are real.'

Summing Up

Before you try for a baby . . .

- Check you're both eating and drinking healthily.

- If your partner isn't already taking a folic acid supplement, encourage her to start right away.

- Plan coming off contraception, and continue to use condoms for a while if your partner's been using the combined pill.

- If your partner is taking any prescription medication, check that it's safe to take for women trying to get pregnant.

Once she's pregnant . . .

- Continue to eat and drink healthily. Encourage your partner to cut out alcohol completely in the first three months.

- Make sure she's taking at least 40mcg (micrograms) of folic acid daily.

- Decide who to tell and when – most couples leave it until after the 12-week scan before announcing the pregnancy.

- Start saving.

- If you're in work, start thinking about paternity/maternity leave.

- Book your first appointment with the midwife/doctor.

Chapter Two

The Pregnancy

From the moment sperm meets egg, to the birth of a full-term baby is a mere 38 weeks! When you think of the miracle that each and every new life is, that's nothing short of amazing. Inevitably, the process isn't always straightforward and things can sometimes go wrong. But on average there are over 600,000 healthy babies born in the UK every year, so the odds are heavily stacked in your favour.

Your partner

During pregnancy your partner's body will be working a lot harder than usual. There's more blood pumping around there for a start, and with her heart working overtime she'll probably feel more tired than usual. Try and lighten the load for her whenever you can; it'll help both her and your unborn baby.

The first trimester

The pregnancy is divided into three periods called 'trimesters'. Weeks 0-12 are known as the first trimester and the baby is developing faster now than at any other stage of the pregnancy. It'll come as no surprise then that your partner will probably be feeling at her worst during this stage of the pregnancy. In particular, morning sickness (which despite its name can occur at any time of the day or night!) is likely to be causing some discomfort and your partner might also notice that her breasts are larger, more tender and the nipples darker. She's also likely to be extra tired and, as the pregnancy hormones start to flow, more emotional than usual. But by the end of this first period of the pregnancy the baby is as good as made. All the vital organs are in place and even the facial features are discernable. In the six months that follow the first trimester, all the foetus does is grow bigger.

'According to the Office for National Statistics, nearly two thousand babies are born in the UK every day.'

The second trimester

Early in the second trimester (which lasts from 13-27 weeks) your partner should be able to feel the baby's movements in the womb quite regularly. In fact, towards the end of this period she'll probably be asked to keep count of them as a way of monitoring the progress that the baby's making. This can be fun at 5 o'clock in the evening, less so perhaps, at 5 o'clock in the morning. Unfortunately it seems that the active, waking and therefore moving periods of your baby at this stage can bear little resemblance to your own or your partner's waking lives. Some of this, as you'd expect, is because when you're moving around and busy you're less likely to notice such things as tiny foetal movements, but research shows that babies are actually soothed by the mother's movement and activity. So he might just be asleep! All of which means if you want to put your hand on her bump and feel the baby moving, you might have to be prepared to do it either early in the morning or last thing at night.

This is the time when your partner will also start to 'look' pregnant – and some of her clothes will start to feel tight. But it's also the period in many pregnancies when a woman 'blooms': your partner's skin might be clearer, her nails stronger and her hair both thicker and shinier. All the early-pregnancy symptoms – extreme fatigue, nausea – should have begun to disappear and if they haven't then your partner should tell her midwife. The risk of miscarriage is also dramatically reduced, which should make both of you feel better. But what started as a small bump stretching at the waistband of your partner's trousers will have grown to the size of a football by the end of this trimester.

The third trimester

The final third of the pregnancy lasts from week 28 to the birth itself. During this period the baby is laying down its own fat stores and preparing itself for birth. Your partner is likely to be more tired than at any other time as her reserves of energy are being rapidly depleted – both by the calories consumed by the baby and the extra weight she's carrying around. Your partner's hands, feet and ankles might be swollen and she may find it hard to get a good night's sleep. An extra pillow to support her bump might be a good idea.

It's often at this stage that the uterus begins the 'practice' contractions known as 'Braxton Hicks'. In fact these often start much earlier in the pregnancy but go unnoticed. What happens is that your partner's bump will tighten and harden for a few seconds – or sometimes several minutes – as the muscles stretch in readiness for the birth.

Towards the end of this trimester your partner's womb will have grown to 1,000 times its normal size and the baby will weigh about two and a half kilos. All that weight pressing down on your partner's bladder probably means she'll need to go to the loo a lot more often. And when combined with the hormones she's producing it might well make her digestive system less efficient. In short, constipation might be something of a problem. A high-fibre diet and drinking plenty of water should help ease the problem. But then, your partner should be eating healthily anyway . . .

Eating for two

It's a myth that pregnancy automatically means doubling the quantities of food eaten, but many women – naturally – do feel their appetite increasing, especially in the first and second trimesters. However, many women feel they aren't given adequate advice about food and weight gain during pregnancy. A recent poll of 6,226 women conducted jointly by the Royal College of Midwives and the website Netmums found 63% saying that their midwife had not explained obesity issues such as body mass index (BMI) during their first antenatal appointment. Yet carrying excess weight in pregnancy can lead to a woman running an increased risk of developing conditions such as pre-eclampsia and diabetes. Women are also at greater risk of suffering miscarriages, as well as premature births and difficulties in delivery, leading to caesarean sections.

The survey also found almost half the women who responded were worried about their weight during pregnancy but many appeared confused about what their correct weight should be. As always, if you're concerned about any of these issues talk to your health visitor or midwife, or see your GP for advice.

Remember that it's not just how much but *what* your partner eats that is especially important. Things she might benefit from having in her diet include:

- Figs – fibre, more potassium than bananas plus plenty of calcium and iron.
- Broccoli – another good source of calcium, plus it's packed with important vitamins and minerals.
- Lentils – fibre, plus iron and protein.
- Orange juice – vitamin C and folic acid, plus potassium.
- Yoghurt – calcium.

Foods to avoid

Eating sensibly and healthily during pregnancy will mean your partner has to avoid certain foods as well as eating what is good for both her and her growing baby. Some foods might make your partner ill; others can damage the unborn baby. Certain shellfish or soft cheeses, for example, carry a high risk of infection. Others, like liver, contain high proportions of vitamin A which can build up in the mother's body to levels which might harm her unborn baby. Things to avoid include:

- Mould-ripened, soft and unpasteurised cheeses. Some types of cheese, such as Camembert, Brie or Chevre (a type of goats' cheese) are softer and less acidic than other cheeses and can harbour potentially dangerous bacteria. Also avoid soft blue cheeses, which are made with mould and can therefore contain listeria – a bacteria that causes a type of food poisoning especially dangerous to unborn children.
- Pâté. Not only does pâté frequently contain high amounts of vitamin A, even vegetable pâté can contain listeria too.
- Marlin, shark and swordfish, all of which have been found to have high levels of mercury which can harm the unborn child's developing nervous system. Children under the age of 16 should also avoid eating such fish and you might sometimes be advised to keep tuna to a minimum for the same reason.

- Raw eggs. Eggs must be fully cooked for anyone who is pregnant, and dishes that use raw or partially-cooked eggs (like carbonara, for example) should be avoided in order to reduce the risk of salmonella or campylobacter. Neither of these types of food poisoning will harm the baby, but they will make your partner ill and therefore are worth avoiding during pregnancy.

- Rare meat. Raw or undercooked meat also carries a high risk of salmonella infection, and you should make sure all meat and meat products are thoroughly cooked and are steaming hot throughout.

- Liver, liver products and vitamin A supplements. You should avoid eating liver and such things as pâté (see previous page) and avoid taking supplements containing vitamin A or fish liver oils (which contain high levels of vitamin A). Everyone – including pregnant women – needs some vitamin A but having too much in pregnancy can harm unborn babies.

- Raw shellfish, such as oysters, can contain bacteria and viruses and should therefore be avoided. But if such food is cooked (thoroughly) it should be perfectly safe, and shellfish rarely carries a high risk of catching listeriosis.

That's quite a list, but it's worth pointing out that listeria infections in the UK among pregnant women are very rare, affecting only about one in 25,000 people. And processed soft cheese and cheese spreads are perfectly safe, as are all hard cheeses. Indeed, they're a vital source of calcium – a very important part of any pregnant woman's diet.

Alcohol

You'll know by now about the importance of reducing alcohol consumption while you and your partner are trying to get pregnant. But your partner needs to continue watching her alcohol intake once she's pregnant. Foetal alcohol syndrome is a condition that can seriously affect the development of the unborn baby, and for this reason the advice usually given is either to avoid alcohol completely or cut down consumption to no more than one or two units per week. Excessive alcohol consumption can also increase the risk of miscarriage, so it is vitally important to be careful.

Smoking

If you or your partner smokes, it is seriously worth trying very, very hard to kick the habit. There can never be a better time, not just for your own sake, but for the sake of your unborn child. Of course, it's never easy. But smoking in pregnancy is known to increase the risk of the foetus developing abnormally as well as raising the likelihood of some early childhood diseases including Sudden Infant Death Syndrome (SIDS). Clearly, if your partner smokes the damage is likely to be greater, but if you smoke you're putting your unborn child – and partner – at greater risk too.

Pre-eclampsia

Around 5% of women suffer from this condition, which is a disorder that only occurs in pregnancy or just after birth. Symptoms can include swelling, headaches and sudden weight gain and it will need urgent attention, often hospitalisation. One reason why blood pressure is monitored and urine samples taken regularly during pregnancy is that both can be an early-warning of this condition, which can be fatal if untreated.

Maternity leave

New mothers can choose to take up to 26 weeks of ordinary maternity leave and 26 weeks of additional maternity leave, regardless of how long they have been with their employer, how many hours they work or how much they are paid, as long as they meet certain notification criteria.

New mothers don't have to take all their entitlement. By law they cannot go back to work in the first two weeks after the baby has been born, or for four weeks if they work in a factory. Otherwise it is up to the individual how long they take but – if she's in work – your partner will need to start planning her time off and notifying her employer. There's more detail about this in a later chapter.

Tests for Down's Syndrome

A relatively new early-pregnancy test called the nuchal scan (either done on its own at about ten weeks or together with the first ultrasound scan in week twelve) measures the thickness of the baby's neck, in particular the nuchal pad. If this is thicker than normal it could be a sign of an increased risk of Down's syndrome, in which case you and your partner will be offered another test called an amniocentesis. This takes place around week 15 and is a more invasive procedure which involves testing a small amount of amniotic fluid. This, naturally, brings with it the risk of a miscarriage and there is now a new way of testing for Down's syndrome by taking a sample of blood, rather than amniotic fluid. You will be advised by your midwife what – if any – tests you both need to think about, and remember – it is your decision.

If the tests show that your unborn baby is at higher risk you'll be talked through the options available, which may include abortion. But if you and your partner decide to proceed with the pregnancy you'll still need to prepare for the birth of your baby in the same way every parent does. Your baby will need exactly the same equipment such as a pram, cot, nappies and clothes. He or she will need the same love, care and attention and be no less of a person. You and your partner will still have to learn all about labour and birth and think about your preferences in terms of pain relief, positions and partner(s). And you will have done all these things if you choose to attend the same antenatal classes that every parent can attend.

Of course, in the years following the birth, your baby will need specialist care and attention, a need likely to continue well into adulthood. But knowing in advance that your baby is going to be born with a condition such as Down's syndrome will at least give you both time to adjust to the news, and find out as much as possible and learn what to expect.

Help and support is available. Your GP or midwife will probably recommend some good sources of information, and the website: www.downs-syndrome.org.uk is also extremely helpful. There is also a book in this series that may help. Take a look at *Down's Syndrome – A Parent's Guide* (Need2Know).

Your baby

Your baby begins as a unique mixture of DNA – yours and your partner's. Just one of the many million sperm you ejaculated will have fertilised the egg and from then on the process of creating the baby begins. The ovum (egg) travels down the fallopian tube – dividing as it does so into a rapidly multiplying cluster of tiny cells – to the uterus. There it attaches itself to the lining of the womb with what are known as 'villi' – strands that help the egg to implant in the endometrium (womb lining) and which will form the basis of the placenta. This vital organ will then ensure that the growing embryo is nourished and sustained throughout the pregnancy. The placenta transfers all the necessary vitamins and minerals from mother to baby via the umbilical tube, while the foetus itself is encased in a fluid-filled membrane called the amniotic sac. This membrane – filled with amniotic fluid – provides a safe and sterile environment for growth and will remain home to the baby for the entire nine months of pregnancy. As the oxygen needed is provided by your partner's blood, the baby swallows and 'breathes' the amniotic fluid quite happily until your partner's waters break and the birth begins.

'Talk about brain power – she'll be growing grey matter at the rate of 250,000 cells per minute!'

Weeks 1-12

At this early stage, of course, the developing baby isn't really a baby at all and is referred to as an embryo. Only by week eight or nine is it officially regarded as a foetus. But by then the bump-to-be (there'll be nothing yet for you and your partner to see!) will have already produced all the specialist cells that will begin to form the heart, lungs, liver, kidneys, nervous system, bones, muscles and blood. Yet at this stage it is still no bigger than a kidney bean – and will also probably look like one! It will weigh just a few grams and the head will make up almost half the overall size. There will even be the buds of future teeth, follicles of hair and – if she's a girl – all the rudimentary germ cells of the ova (eggs) she'll ripen and release monthly as a woman. And talk about brain power – she'll be growing grey matter at the rate of 250,000 cells per minute!

Weeks 13-27

It's at about this time that your partner will start to look and feel pregnant. But as the foetus grows, so does your partner's womb. At week 13 the foetus is about as long as a human thumb and although it's still tiny, it is now much stronger and less likely to succumb to neo-natal infections. By week 15 the foetus is about the size of a pear but a lot more active! Your partner will almost certainly start to notice movements, as well as feeling when the baby gets the hiccups. By the end of this period, your baby will be able to hear sounds and recognise the sound of your and your partner's voices. So talk to her! Play her some music: some people recommend a bit of Mozart, but there's no conclusive evidence that it makes any difference either to intelligence or the future baby's taste in music. By week 27 the baby will probably weigh over 500 grams and be almost 30 centimetres long.

Weeks 28-40

In this last phase of the pregnancy, the baby will pile on the weight as her skeleton hardens, her head gets bigger and she starts to lay down fat reserves to keep her warm and see her through the birth. But as she gets larger, so the space to move around becomes restricted and by week 32 or thereabouts many babies will already be in the 'head down' position ready for birth. But she can still kick, and with stronger limbs those moves might hurt. In spite of the limited space, your partner should still be feeling around ten such movements in every 12-hour period.

From early in the pregnancy the baby has been covered, as it floated in the amniotic fluid, by a creamy substance known as vernix. (Think cross-Channel swimmers covered in grease, and for a similar reason.) But soon both this and the downy hair (lanugo) that covers a baby in the womb will start to disappear – another sure sign that things are gearing up for what's about to happen. In fact, by week 36 your partner's pregnancy is medically 'full-term' even though her due date is still about four weeks away. As the birth approaches, the baby's head should 'engage' in your partner's pelvic cavity – shielded and protected by her bones in much the same way as a cycle helmet!

You

Although all the really exciting things might be happening to your partner, there's plenty for you to do as the big day approaches. For a start, you need to be prepared to help out as much as possible in the home. Shopping, cleaning, cooking, dusting, anything you can do to make life easy will be helping both your partner and your baby. It should be clear by now that your partner's body is undergoing one of the most profound and taxing changes ever undertaken. She will naturally be tired; she might be irritable and/or emotional; she needs you to be there and to understand.

There is a rather fanciful idea that some men suffer sympathetic symptoms of their partner's pregnancy. This phenomenon – called Couvade – can mean dads-to-be suffering anything from morning sickness to Braxton Hicks contractions and up to 25% of dads report sharing some of their partner's pain quite literally. How – or indeed, why – this should be is anyone's guess, but it is certainly true that male hormones do respond to being in the vicinity of pregnant women. Something in your body is changing, if only to prepare you for the role of being a dad.

'Up to 25% of dads report sharing some of their partner's pain quite literally.'

The nursery

Men, it's said, love a project. That's why we're more likely to mow the lawns even if that's the only gardening we do. And there is plenty to be getting on with before the birth, not least preparing a bedroom for the new addition. During the first few weeks and months most babies share a bedroom with their parents, but a time will come when, for everyone's sake, Mum and Dad need to be left alone. Decide early what your options are. That way you can buy furniture, assemble it, re-decorate and whatever else that you decide needs doing while you've still got the time and energy. If you know the sex of your offspring, you can even choose an appropriate colour scheme and decorations. If not, something neutral will suffice. And there's another good reason for getting it done now, while you can. You don't want to subject your baby's delicate lungs to paint fumes as soon as he gets home.

'You' time

No matter how well prepared you are, how much reading you've done and how much you've both talked it through, you'll still be amazed at how different your life was when it was simply 'you and her'. So set aside some time before the birth to do the things that you enjoy together; spend time enjoying each other's company while you've both still got the energy! And catch up with old friends. Although you might find you are inundated with requests to visit after your child's been born, they're coming to see the baby, not you. And you might just want to say 'no' for a while until you both adjust to your new responsibilities. So seeing friends, sharing a meal or a trip to the cinema or having people to stay beforehand can be good for everyone.

Sex and pregnancy

There's an awful lot of nonsense written about sex and pregnancy. While in the early days and weeks your partner might not feel up to it and later on it might become something of a physical challenge, there is no biological reason why it can't be done. Your partner will have stopped ovulating, so there's no chance of her developing another pregnancy. (Don't laugh – I have been asked!) As always, though, you need to put your partner first. Don't make excessive demands and do be prepared to consider other ways of being intimate.

The oft-cited pearl that having sex can bring on the birth might, however, contain a grain of truth. Semen contains quite high amounts of prostaglandin, a hormone used as part of the process of inducing babies when they're overdue. Similarly, it's sometimes said that stimulating the nipples can trigger the onset of labour. Old wives' tale? Should you get near enough to do this, you might find out for yourself. But as it's unlikely, be satisfied with the knowledge that your partner's breasts are preparing to do what they were made to do: namely, feed the baby. And, if nothing else, having sex helps pass the time.

'The oft-cited pearl that having sex can bring on the birth might, however, contain a grain of truth.'

Paternity leave

At the time of writing, dads are entitled to a mere two weeks statutory paternity leave, although there are plans to increase this by sharing some of the woman's maternity entitlement. Paternity leave has to be taken as two consecutive weeks rather than odd days here or there and must be completed within 56 days of the birth, although some employers may be more generous. You're entitled to receive £123.06 a week, or 90% of your average weekly earnings.

Antenatal classes

'We went to the antenatal classes at the hospital. They were pretty good to be fair, although because my wife chose a hospital away from where we lived we didn't meet any new friends for us, as it were.'

Richard, father to Gwendolen, 12 months.

Around week 32 you and your partner will probably be given the chance to attend antenatal or parent craft classes. Those run by your local NHS Trust will be free; others, such as those provided by the National Childbirth Trust (NCT) make a small charge. The choice of which to attend – or whether to attend at all – is yours, although if your partner decides that she'd like to go you should make every effort to accompany her. The things covered by these classes – like pain relief during labour and the different types of birth available – are important to you both. Having you there will help make sure the information is available when it's most needed – at the birth – and not forgotten amid all the excitement. Remember, by then your partner will have other things on her mind.

As well as being taught about the physical process of pregnancy and birth, if you attend NHS classes at your local hospital you'll probably be given a tour of the maternity unit. It's useful to see for yourself (assuming that you have both opted for a hospital birth) where things are likely to happen. It can reduce the stress when the time comes.

But perhaps the most important reason you need to be there is so that you can learn the breathing, relaxation and pain relief techniques that your partner will be using. In particular, you – or whoever she chooses as her birth partner – need to know what you can do to help ease the pain during the process of labour. You might also pick up some useful tips on performing gentle massage as your partner goes into labour.

Finally, you'll be talked through the various options available, from home births to water births, as well as being given advice on breastfeeding and some vital tips on caring for your newborn baby. You'll be asked to make a birth plan detailing some of the decisions you've made about the birth and the kind of pain relief your partner thinks she'd like. And you might find, being in the company of people in the same position, that new friendships emerge as experiences, anxieties and hopes are shared.

Summing Up

- Ensure both you and your partner are eating and drinking healthily throughout the pregnancy – in her case, for the sake of the baby and in your case because you'll need to be on top of your game when he arrives!

- Find out about the antenatal classes that are running in your area. Talk to other mums and dads about which ones they found most useful, and book yourself on to one of the courses.

- Make sure you sort out as much as you can before the baby arrives. Decide where he or she is going to sleep and prepare the room accordingly. Start to think about the length of maternity and paternity leave you both require, and talk to your employers.

Chapter Three

Birth

Preparing for the birth

Birth can be a difficult, painful affair and no matter how prepared you and your partner are, it pays to keep going over those small but vital details. Look again at your birth plan and decide if it's still appropriate. As the pregnancy progresses your partner might feel more apprehensive about what's ahead and change her mind. And this might happen often. Remind her of the reasons for choosing the plan you both selected; discuss whatever factors are persuading her to change her mind; reassure her that you love her and you'll be there for her – and if the birth plan has to change it has to change.

Your partner

There are several basic signs that your partner might be going into labour:

- She might start suffering from persistent lower back pain as the baby moves lower into the pelvic region. Some women actually find breathing a little easier when this happens, and it's sometimes known as 'lightening' for that reason.

- Her breasts might enlarge as they prepare for breastfeeding, and the nipples darken and harden.

- A 'show' or brownish, blood-tinged mucus discharge. This is the 'plug' that blocks the cervix, preventing bacteria entering the uterus and losing it might be a sign that labour is starting. It's certainly a sign that things are happening, although labour might still be several days away.

'Birth can be a difficult, painful affair and no matter how prepared you and your partner are, it pays to keep going over those small but vital details.'

- Practice contractions, known as 'Braxton Hicks', which are merely a warm-up act for the real thing and relatively painless.

- Waters breaking. Towards the end of pregnancy the amniotic sac filled with the fluid that protects and cushions the baby will burst. If this happens at anything after week 36 it's a sure sign that labour is happening. It can occur earlier in the pregnancy and if it does, your partner should see her GP/midwife immediately as the baby may be at greater risk of infection.

- Dilation of the cervix. The cervix really is the door to what's about to happen, and when it starts dilating, it means the door is opening. But it is frequently slow-going, and it's not uncommon for it to take several hours before it's fully dilated.

If this is her first pregnancy, your partner might not be as aware of some or all the signs as she would be if it had happened to her before. But all pregnancies are different, and that certainly goes for the onset of labour. So be on the lookout. Keep in touch with the hospital or midwife – and don't be embarrassed by any 'false alarms'.

Pain management

Once labour is well and truly underway, you'll be on your way to the hospital (if you've opted for a hospital delivery, that is) if only to let your partner have access to some of the pain-management facilities as the contractions become more uncomfortable. You will probably both have learnt about all the standard pain-management procedures at the antenatal classes you attended. And you will hopefully understand your role in reminding her – at vital moments – of what she's learnt and what decisions you both have made.

What's available, and what you use, is of course a personal choice. But some of the alternatives will be more appropriate at different stages of your partner's labour, so it's worth examining them.

'I don't suppose anything can really prepare you for the birth, and certainly nothing can fully prepare you for actually having a child, but at least the antenatal classes gave me at least some idea of what to do (and what not to do) at the appropriate times!'

Richard, father to Gwendolen, 12 months

The first stage of labour

This is often the longest part of the entire process. The cervix isn't yet fully dilated (open) and yet contractions have started as the uterus prepares to push the baby down the birth canal.

As the contractions gradually become stronger, they'll become harder to endure and your partner might need you to remind her of some of the relaxation and breathing techniques she was probably taught at the antenatal classes. Many women find lying in a warm bath helps ease the pain, but if neither of those options is sufficient your partner might be offered use of a TENS machine. A TENS (Transcutaneous Electrical Nerve Stimulation) machine works by emitting small electrical impulses to the body through small pads attached to your partner's back. These impulses are thought to stimulate the release of endorphins – the body's natural pain-management and 'feel-good' chemicals, although it's by no means certain. Some suggest instead that the TENS machine blocks the pain receptors and prevents them travelling up the spinal cord to the brain. What is certain is that TENS works well for some women in the early stages of labour, and many women buy or hire them for use at home before travelling to the hospital.

The second stage of labour

Once the cervix is fully dilated, the second stage of labour has officially started. By now the contractions are both stronger and closer together, the urge to 'push' is overwhelming and levels of discomfort and pain can become so acute that – in spite of any earlier protestations about resisting medical intervention – your partner may want to avail herself of any one of the pain-management procedures available. These include:

- Entonox, also known as 'gas and air'. Literally nitrous oxide (laughing gas) and oxygen, this helps temporarily block the brain's pain receptors but takes a minute or so to take effect. This means your partner will need to inhale (through a mask or mouthpiece) as soon as she feels a contraction so that – when it reaches its peak – the entonox can take effect.

- Pethidine. This is a member of the opium family of drugs. That fact alone should tell you something about its pain-relieving properties. It often creates feelings of intoxication, and some women don't like the feelings of being 'drunk' or 'tipsy'. It's usually given by injection, and lasts for several hours but it can cross the placenta and affect the baby so it needs to be used carefully. Pethidine is not recommended if labour is likely to be short (say, less than four hours).

- Epidural. This involves inserting a needle into the spine and administering drugs through a catheter into the spinal cord. This blocks transmission of signals through the nerves in or near the spinal column and therefore reduces the pain and dulls some of the sensations below the waist. Although very effective as a means of controlling the pain, this can sometimes cause the second stage of labour to last longer.

By this stage the head will almost certainly have fully engaged in your partner's pelvic area – and there's no going back. At the same time, the midwife will probably start encouraging your partner to push even harder, as well as shouting things like 'I can see the baby's head!' And she probably can. But no matter how hard she feels she has been pushing up to now, you'll need to encourage your partner to put in a near-Herculean effort to help move the baby down the birth canal and out into the world.

This second stage can last anything from half an hour to two or more hours, and it's important for your partner to try and synchronise her pushes with each of the contractions, and not to push at all when they subside. In all the confusion and pain, the urge to push and get it over with can be overwhelming. You should encourage your partner to pant rather than push when the contractions subside. And the midwife will probably want to slow things down a little once the baby has 'crowned' (its head has appeared) in order to allow the vaginal wall to stretch and reduce the risk of tearing. On the other hand, he or she may well decide an episiotomy is necessary. This is when a small cut is made to widen the vaginal opening and prevent tearing.

Once the baby's head has been delivered, you'll know things are swiftly moving to their conclusion. Keep talking to your partner, reassuring her and telling her what's happening. She'll probably not be able to see for herself. Some men even bring a small mirror with them so that they can show the baby's head to their partner. But try not to get in the way. Just a few more pushes are probably all that will be necessary to complete the delivery.

Skin-to-skin contact

Once the baby is born it will almost certainly be handed to your partner for some important skin-to-skin bonding. Be patient; you'll get to hold your son or daughter in a moment. It's important that mother and child are together in this way: it calms the baby after what must have been, in all honesty, a rather shocking experience. And it will give your partner a useful rush of a hormone called prolactin, which not only helps stimulate breast feeding but is also one of the hormones responsible for the feelings of pleasure and relaxation which follow sexual stimulation. I'm sure you'll agree she could do with a little something to help her feel good after all that hard work. And as if that wasn't enough, the good news is that breast feeding then helps with the third and final stage of labour.

The third stage of labour

The final stage of labour is the delivery of the placenta. Naturally, this process might take up to an hour although – as you've just read – if your partner is breastfeeding nature has a wonderful way of speeding things along a little. In most cases your partner will probably have been offered an injection, which is given at the moment the baby is born and this usually means that the placenta – or 'afterbirth' – is ejected fairly quickly. Your job will be to hold the baby!

Your baby

If all has gone to plan, your baby will have made his or her appearance entirely unassisted, without suffering any trauma or distress. On the other hand, being squeezed out of the safety and warmth of the womb, down the birth canal and out into a world of lights, people and noise can't be all that pleasant. So it's hardly surprising that – sometimes – babies need a little gentle encouragement to make an appearance.

'You'll need to encourage your partner to put in a near-Herculean effort to help move the baby down the birth canal and out into the world.'

Forceps and ventouse delivery

Approximately one in every eight births will require some sort of help with the delivery. A long labour might have tired the mother to the point that she can no longer push effectively; she might be unable to push due to having a heart condition or the pushing might be causing distress to the baby. Either way, a couple of simple procedures can help your baby make a slightly overdue appearance. Forceps are like large stainless steel sugar tongs which surround the baby's head so that it can be gently cradled while the doctor or midwife gently pulls the baby out. If the baby is in the breech position (legs and bottom first) forceps might be needed once the baby's body has been delivered. Either way, using forceps often means your partner having an episiotomy (small cut) in the vaginal wall in order to insert the forceps round the baby's head. So if a little extra pressure is all that is required, a ventouse delivery is often preferable. This involves a small rubber cap which is attached to a vacuum device being placed on the baby's head. By applying gentle suction the baby can be delivered quickly and without the need for even the most minor surgery.

Caesarean births

About one in four births in the UK are by what is called caesarean section. This is a surgical procedure, and involves making an incision through the abdomen and into the womb. Obviously this is done under anaesthetic, although sometimes this needn't be general. It will depend why the operation is thought necessary, and in some cases your partner will know beforehand that she's going to give birth this way. In others it will be decided at some stage during the labour.

Making sure the baby is okay

In the hours after your baby's birth you will probably be offered a series of tests to check his general health and development. This is all routine, and is done to make sure everything is working normally. A doctor or midwife will probably carry out a brief physical examination of the baby (sometimes called an Apgar test) in the first few minutes after he or she is born which involves:

34

- Listening to the heartbeat.

- Testing reflexes.

- Checking skin colour, muscle tone and respiration.

In addition, someone will probably offer to do a hearing test and a heel-prick test (involving taking two or three drops of the baby's blood from the heel) before your baby comes home. The heel-prick test is sometimes called a Guthrie test and screens for several rare conditions, including one called PKU (phenylketonuria). It's also normal for the baby to be weighed and measured shortly after birth.

Some newborn babies have a condition called jaundice. This is quite common and is simply caused by high levels of bilirubin in the blood. It might make your baby sleepy, and you might notice a slightly yellow tinge to the skin.

In very rare cases a baby can be born with a condition called haemorrhagic disease which prevents the blood clotting. This can lead to uncontrolled spontaneous bleeding. If the bleeding is seen (for example, if the baby starts bleeding from the nose) the condition can be treated and the bleeding stopped. But if it occurs out of sight, say in the brain, it can lead to permanent physical and mental impairment. For this reason the Department of Health recommends that, shortly after birth, all babies are given a vitamin K supplement either in the form of an injection or by mouth. You and your partner will be asked about this during antenatal appointments, and you'll need to have made your decision by the time of the birth itself.

Breastfeeding

Newborn infants have a powerful instinct to suck – anything and everything they can get their lips round. You might have found that out already if you've let your finger get too close. But the sucking a newborn baby does is not quite what people imagine. For a start, a baby doesn't so much suck the breast with the lips (as you might have done!) as make an attempt to swallow it. His mouth will open wide and – rather like a sink plunger – create a vacuum over as much of the nipple and surrounding tissue as possible. This 'latching on' as it's called, can take a bit of getting used to and is by no means as easy as it sounds. Many of the women who give up breastfeeding (and although most try it, figures suggest that only half still breastfeed at six months) will do so because this latching on process is uncomfortable or painful, inefficient or all three. And part of the reason is that the milk doesn't just come out of a single central hole; the nipple is more like a shower head than a tap.

If your partner has decided that she'd like to breastfeed she'll be encouraged in the moments following the birth to get the baby 'latched on'. If not, and she'd like to use a bottle, the hospital will provide one. There's no doubt 'breast is best' but it isn't always enough. There's a reason why the rate of infant mortality in the West has plummeted in the last 100 years, and it sometimes helps to remember that formula doesn't mean that anyone's a failure.

You

After reading the above, you might be wondering what – if anything – is left for you to do. Your partner and the baby are the stars of this particular show, and the focus of everyone's attention will be on them. Of course, if you attended antenatal classes with your partner and you were present at the birth you'll have played your part. Many women find the presence of their partner a great comfort, especially in an unfamiliar hospital environment. Mind you, she might not show it. Be prepared to hear the kind of language not normally associated with that gorgeous feminine creature you adore. And it doesn't mean that she adores you any the less. Don't take it personally.

Instead, get on with the business of giving her a massage, reminding her about her breathing exercises, conveying the midwife's instructions in case she can't hear them and telling her how wonderful she's being and how well she's coping. Even if she isn't.

Letting people know

In the excitement of the birth it's easy to overlook the needs of family and friends who'll probably all be waiting eagerly to hear the news. Now would not be the time to find that your mobile isn't charged (although you'll probably find you've got to leave the labour ward to use it) or that you haven't got someone's phone number. A useful strategy is to arrange beforehand for a sort of telephone-buddy system, whereby you text or phone the most important people (I'll leave you to decide who they might be) and they, in turn, let other friends or members of the family know.

Going home

You will. And it will probably be late. You might have been awake for hours. But you might also find you can't possibly sleep. What should you do? If it's the middle of the night, no one short of an antipodean friend or relation is going to thank you for phoning them. So why not make yourself useful? Get cooking. Get out all your pots and pans and prepare as many things as you can for when your partner and new baby get home. The easier you can make it, the better. Put meals in the freezer, then you've got them when you want them. The last thing you'll have the time or energy for is cooking. And it can be a useful way to use up all that surplus nervous energy.

Car safety

Of course, your partner might not want to stay in hospital a moment longer than she has to. And even if she does, the time will soon come when you'll have to arrange for transport home. It's vital that your new baby is carried safely if you're travelling by car, and this means getting a suitable car seat. Some hospitals even have a policy of ensuring that you have one and know how to use it before they'll let you travel home with your new baby. What to buy and how to fit it will be something that you'll have decided long before the moment that it's necessary to use it. Suffice to say there are a range of options, from stand-alone car seats (you need one suitable from birth) to entire travel systems which combine both pushchair, car seat and sometimes carrycot as well. Just make sure that what you buy conforms to the new United Nations Standards ECE R44.03 and R44.04. In some cases the old British Standards are still legal, but it's wise to go for something based on the very latest research into child car safety. And never buy one second hand. It might look fine, but could have invisible damage only likely to become apparent in the case of a collision.

Summing Up

As your partner approaches her due date, it's worth taking the time to pack a bag to take with you to the hospital. You don't want to have to do this in a hurry, at the last minute. Things to include are:

For the baby:

- A pack of nappies suitable for a newborn.
- Some muslin cloths.
- Clothes: a pack of all-in-one sleepsuits plus something warm (including hat) for coming home.

For your partner:

- Maternity pads, breast pads and a nursing bra.
- A change of clothes. It might be advisable to take things that are comfortable but old for your partner to wear when in labour.
- Nightwear, slippers, dressing gown and towel (if staying overnight).
- Snacks and drinks.
- Music – some favourite CDs, perhaps. Most delivery rooms will have a CD player.
- Maternity notes, including birth plan.

For you:

- A camera, with charged batteries and film/memory card.
- A book to read. Labour can sometimes be a long, drawn-out affair.
- Phone, plus all the numbers that you're likely to need.
- Snacks and drinks.

Chapter Four

First Days and Months

Life is about to change forever. If this is your first child nothing will ever be quite the same again. Where before there may have been just two of you, now there are (at least) three: and two of them – your partner and your baby – are going to need all the help they can get. So are you. You're going to have to do some adjusting and it's important to know what's happening and why so that you can understand better what it means to be a father.

Looking after a newborn baby is a full-time, 24-hour occupation. If it's your first child everything will be new and wonderful, as well as slightly terrifying. All this is perfectly normal. There will be times when you gaze at your baby and feel on top of the world; there will be others when you wonder what on earth you've both done. Life has changed forever. Sleep – what you get of it – will be disrupted and you will probably both feel more tired than you ever thought was possible. So put yourselves and the baby first. You may be inundated with visitors and requests to see the new arrival. If you can fit them in, fine. But if you and your partner are just too tired, say so. Give yourselves the time and space to get used to the way your life has changed.

Your partner

Giving birth isn't always a traumatic test of extreme endurance. Some women find it relatively straightforward (compared to other mums). But it is never easy. It helps to have learned as much as you can before the birth, and to have made decisions together. If your partner feels she's in control it can help ease the process of labour tremendously. But remember that – however well you've both coped – your partner has just undergone one of the most stressful, memorable, frightening and exhausting times of her life. Let her talk to you about it; ask her how she's feeling. No matter how many times you've heard it

'We wanted a home birth for Noah. I was initially unsure, but after attending a couple of home birth classes felt a lot happier about it. It seems to be a much more relaxing experience for mum and baby.'

Ben, father-of-two and author of *Goodbye, Pert Breasts: The Diary of a Newborn Dad.*

before, it can be therapeutic for your partner, especially if it was a difficult birth. She'll need a lot of understanding, care and attention from you in the days and months following the birth of your baby.

Her body

It may be that your partner has some pretty serious physical wear and tear to recover from. Then there's the sheer energy she's just spent getting the latest member of your family into the world. A natural (or vaginal) birth may have resulted in tearing and bleeding, or even deliberate cutting (episiotomy) to give the baby more room to get out. These may need stitches. If your partner has had a caesarean birth there will be the anaesthetic, as well as the surgery, to recover from. Assuring her that you still find her beautiful (without applying pressure for sex) is very important at this time.

'You need to be prepared to step up to the mark and pretty much take on the cooking, cleaning, shopping . . . '

People are different, and some mums are up and about quite soon after giving birth; others take time to get over the experience. Either way, your partner may find she is physically incapable of doing things like household chores. You need to be prepared to step up to the mark and pretty much take on the cooking, cleaning, shopping and general dogsbodying as well as doing your fair share of nappy-changing.

Breastfeeding

If your partner is breastfeeding this will be another physical demand on her body. The process of producing milk takes vital energy and means it's important to eat and drink sensibly. Alcohol intake should be low or non-existent as it can pass into breast milk as well as lead to dehydration. Keeping up your partner's fluid intake is essential, for obvious reasons. Ensuring she has access to regular, healthy meals is also vital.

Weight loss

By the end of the first month following the birth your partner's weight should be beginning to return to normal. Mums who breastfeed will almost always return to their normal weight sooner than mums who bottle feed, for obvious reasons.

Some mums, however, struggle to lose the weight they've gained during pregnancy. And seeing celebrity mums who regain their slender figure in a few weeks (thanks, no doubt, to a team of nannies plus personal trainer) can heap enormous pressure on a mother at an already vulnerable time. Be aware that little things you say or do can either help enormously or make a difficulty even harder.

Most women are body-conscious to some extent, and the chances are your partner won't be given much by way of medical advice about the issue of weight loss after pregnancy. A recent survey of over 6,000 women by the Royal College of Midwives found that six out of 10 felt under pressure to lose weight quickly after giving birth. The same survey also found that 84% of women said the advice they received from midwives on weight management both during and after pregnancy was inadequate.

While excess weight both during and after pregnancy can lead to a range of potential health problems, living in a world that worships the body beautiful isn't exactly helping anyone either. The sad fact is that many perfectly healthy women have an excessively negative view of their body. At the same time, advice is sometimes difficult to come by. A spokesman from the Department of Health said this in response to the issues raised in the Royal College of Midwives' survey: 'It is crucial that mothers get the support they need before, during and after birth and we are working with the Royal College of Midwives, the NHS and others to make this happen. Health visitors have a key role in making sure that all mothers and babies get advice about what to eat, exercise and lifestyle . . . [and] we are committed to recruiting an extra 4,200 health visitors.'

'A recent survey of over 6,000 women by the Royal College of Midwives found that six out of 10 felt under pressure to lose weight quickly after giving birth.'

Emotions

Your partner might also be emotional in the days and weeks after the birth. One of the most miraculous things to ever happen has just happened to her; a new human being has been born and now depends on her for its survival. The responsibility can be overwhelming. Add to that the huge changes in hormone levels your partner will be having and you need to prepare for a roller-coaster ride. There will be tears of joy but also tears of rage and fatigue and anger and frustration. It's normal. You need to understand that your partner probably can't help it (any more than you) and be as supportive as you can.

Postnatal depression

The hormonal, chemical and emotional changes that follow the birth of a baby can sometimes develop into something more serious than mere 'baby blues'. Postnatal depression is the term given to a condition which may affect as many as one in ten women. Occurring two to eight weeks after delivery, postnatal depression is more than merely feeling extra tired or unhappy: it is a medical condition and requires treatment. Symptoms can include:

- Anxiety.
- Loss of appetite.
- Panic attacks.
- Irritability.
- Insomnia.
- Lethargy.

Having one or more of the above is not necessarily a sign of depression; there are few people who haven't suffered from at least some of the above from time to time. But having such symptoms for a sustained period or having them to extremes means it might be worth your partner getting checked out. Although the doctor, midwife or health visitor should ask your partner how she's feeling following the birth of your child and be on the look out for symptoms, postnatal depression can be difficult to diagnose and your partner might be reluctant to admit to such feelings. Do all you can to encourage your partner to tell the doctor how she's feeling so that if she needs any help, she can get it. Taking a look at *Postnatal Depression – The Essential Guide* (Need2Know) may help too.

And men, it seems, can sometimes suffer too. A recent US study found that between 10-25% of men suffered from postnatal depression. And although we haven't been through the physical mill like our partners, it is worth remembering that our hormones are affected by merely being near pregnant women and new mothers, so there may well be a physical reason behind male postnatal depression.

The postnatal check

Around six weeks after the birth your partner should be given an opportunity to talk to a doctor about her health and wellbeing. This could be back at the hospital where she gave birth, or with your local GP. This is an important opportunity to discuss her physical wellbeing following the birth as well as her feelings and emotions. Routines vary, but the postnatal check usually includes the following:

- A check of your partner's weight. A lot of women are sensitive about this following the birth of a child, but it's important to find out whether your partner is returning to her pre-pregnancy weight.

- A blood test and blood pressure measurement.

- A urine test to make sure your partner's kidneys are working properly.

- A physical examination. This is likely to be the most uncomfortable part of the check but if your partner has had stitches the doctor will need to know if they have healed and whether the uterus has returned to its normal size.

'A recent US study found that between 10-25% of men suffered from postnatal depression.'

You

You need to be able to support your partner in whatever ways you can as she recovers from the birth and adjusts to the routine of a newborn baby. But you've also got some adjusting to do. No matter how well prepared you might have been, how much you anticipated the birth of your child or how ecstatic you feel in the days after the birth, things are going to get tough.

For a start, you'll have to get used to the fact that there's now someone else in your partner's life. You might not get the attention that you're used to getting. It's not uncommon for dads to feel a little jealous of this magical new relationship between mother and baby, especially if you're doing much of the dirty work. And it is dirty. Changing a nappy is never nice, and at first you might be all fingers and thumbs. But it gets easier. You'll get used to the smell and get a lot quicker at it. Some new dads even become quite competitive about it!

'Bath time in particular is a great way for dads to get involved, and it can be fun too.'

Bonding

If you qualify – and have applied for – paternity leave (see chapter 2) you'll be able to spend some time at home with your partner and new baby. It's important to use those first few days and weeks to bond with your new baby.

A lot is written about the importance of mother-baby bonding, but less is said about the importance of dads getting to know and bonding with their baby. Chances are you'll get plenty of time alone with your offspring, if only to give your partner a break. So make the most of it. Bath time in particular is a great way for dads to get involved, and it can be fun too, even with a newborn. Just remember what you were told about bathing in antenatal classes or at the hospital – hold the baby firmly (but not too tightly) in your left arm with your hand under her left shoulder. That way, your arm should support her head and leave your right hand free to do the washing. And enjoy the special splash-time with your little one and – if it fits in with your work and lifestyle – make this time your own.

Changing a nappy

Ok, it might not be particularly pleasant, but someone's got to do it. And that someone might as well be you! Besides, you can put the time to good use, smiling, talking and making eye contact with the little bundle of . . . well, joy. And you might as well get used to nappies. In the first three months you'll be changing in excess of 750 of the things. And in the first year you'll probably change a whopping 2,500 nappies – that's ten per day, so you'll get a lot of practice. Here's how you do it:

- Make sure you've got everything you need to hand: wipes (or water/cotton wool balls); clean nappy; nappy bag and a cloth or an old towel (for accidents).

- Lie your baby on her back on a clean, dry surface (not too high).

- Take off the dirty nappy and put it out of the baby's reach.

- Gently clean the area working from front to back. Again, put the soiled wipes or cotton wool balls out of reach.

- With one hand, take hold of both the baby's legs and lift them slightly.

- Place a clean nappy underneath your baby's bottom.

- Bring the bottom of the nappy up between your baby's legs and fasten, either with the tapes if you're using disposables or grips or pins if using cloth nappies.

Job done!

Making a bottle

Ok, so 'breast is best' as we've already said, but there are times when bottle feeding might be necessary either as a supplement to breast milk or as an alternative. Even if your partner is breastfeeding, you can still give your baby a bottle using milk that she's expressed. But bottle feeding using formula is an area where a dad can really make a difference. And here's how it's done.

- First, make sure you've got everything you need: bottles, formula, and steriliser. It's vital that everything you use is sterilised, and a simple steam steriliser that you can put in the microwave is probably the answer.

- Next, fill the kettle with fresh water and set it to boil. It's important not to re-boil water that's already in the kettle as the concentration of minerals can increase to harmful levels. Some parents use bottled water but this really isn't necessary in the UK. Tap water is fine: just make sure it's fresh.

- Now fill the (sterilised) bottle with the right amount of water. This will vary according to the age of your child and all you need to do is follow the instructions on the formula packet or tin.

- Now, using the scoop provided with the formula, measure precisely the right amount of the feed and drop it onto the surface of the water. The neck of your baby's bottle should be wide enough for you to do this, but take care. It's important that he gets the right quantity of powder to water: too little and he might be hungry; too much and he might get poorly.

- Screw on the lid of the bottle (plus teat) and up-end or gently shake the bottle a few times. This should be enough to mix the formula.

- If you're going to use it straight away, you'll now need to cool the mixture and the easiest way is to stand the bottle in a bowl of cold water. Test the temperature by shaking a couple of drops onto your wrist. If you can feel it then it's still too hot.

- If you're saving the bottle for later, put it straight into the fridge. Of course this means you'll have to warm it up again before using it, in which case do the same as for cooling except this time stand it in a bowl of warm water. Don't be tempted to give it a few seconds in the microwave, as this can heat the formula unevenly and lead to burns.

Registering the birth

All births in the UK have to be officially recorded and it's the parents' responsibility to ensure that this is done within 42 days of the birth. If you fail to register the birth of your child you could incur a fine. It's a straightforward procedure, as straightforward as making an appointment with the registrar, turning up with your baby, your hospital notes and your passports and handing over the fee for a birth certificate. If you and your partner aren't married and you want to be named on the birth certificate as the father (and why wouldn't you?) you'll need to go to the register office together. If your partner goes alone your name cannot appear on your child's birth certificate (as happened to Ed Milliband).

Registration checklist

- The birth of a child has to be registered within 42 days.

- You need to book an appointment at your nearest register office first. You can usually find the number in the Yellow Pages.

- Make sure you both take with you some form of photo identification. A passport is ideal or the photo-card element of your driving licence. In addition, you'll need to have the hospital discharge letter (given to your partner when she and the baby came home).

- The registrar will ask for the forename and surname that you'd like to give the baby, plus details of the date and place of birth. You and your partner will be asked for your full name, date of birth and occupation.

- At the end of the process you'll be given a short birth certificate, which has just the baby's details on. However, to apply for a passport (and remember, babies need their own these days) your child will need a long birth certificate as well, which will cost an extra £3.50.

Play

It might seem like there's not a lot a dad can do with a newborn apart from change her nappy, but there's plenty, most of it silly, and all of it useful. Try . . .

- Blowing raspberries and making silly noises.

- Singing, though not too loudly.

- Gently tickling your baby's feet.

- Stroking her cheek.

- Letting her grab hold of your finger.

But be careful! Babies can have quite a grip, and they're programmed not to let go!

'It might seem like there's not a lot a dad can do with a newborn apart from change her nappy, but there's plenty, most of it silly, and all of it useful.'

Your baby

At this stage your baby has three basic needs: food, sleep and you! It's as simple as that. Babies are born with an in-built survival mechanism, such as the need to suckle. If you stroke your baby's upper lip he will open his mouth; insert the tip of your finger and he will start to suck. No one teaches babies to do that. They do it anyway. It's a basic survival instinct or reflex. Another in-built reflex is the 'stepping' movement which you'll notice if you lift your baby up and hold him over something like a table.

Between birth and three months all babies have these basic reflexes and they are usually tested shortly after a baby is born to make sure everything is working normally. Parenthood at this stage revolves around these basic needs and reflexes. Your baby needs to feed, to be kept warm and clean, to sleep. When holding your baby, you must support the head and neck. This is because the muscles aren't yet strong enough for the baby to support the weight itself.

Milestones

The basic developmental stages in a baby's life are known as milestones. In the first month these milestones include:

- Responding to sounds.
- Smiling.
- Laughing.
- Making noises.

By two months many babies can also:

- Follow objects with their eyes.
- Hold up their heads.
- Bear their weight (with you holding their hands) on their legs.

At three months, your baby might be:

- Holding her head steady.

- Showing signs that she recognises you and your partner.
- Rolling over.

These are just a few of the basic milestones. But don't forget babies don't just grow physically. (If they did, they would merely become adult-sized babies!) Your baby needs to grow intellectually, emotionally and socially as well and this is where play comes in.

Reflexes

From birth, a baby comes pre-programmed to do an astonishing range of things, from smiling to grasping to crawling and even swimming. No doubt there's a good evolutionary reason for each one of these reflex activities, although these days most will disappear after a few weeks only to be re-learned later on. The point is your newborn is more than a milk-consuming, poo factory. For a start, his or her brain is wired to start gathering and processing all the information it can get – and that includes you. You're being watched, and watched intently. What you do has probably never been under such close scrutiny. The things you say and do and even the CDs you play can be heard even while the baby is asleep, so you've got to be careful.

'Your newborn is more than a milk-consuming, poo factory.'

Sleep

In the early days of its life, a baby may sleep for up to 18 hours a day. Even by the end of the third month, she might still only be awake for nine or ten hours each day. And for 'day' read 'twenty-four hour period' because a newborn baby's sleep patterns typically do work in three or four hour cycles. But although they may only stay awake for just a few hours, your baby's brain is working around the clock adjusting and adapting to its new environment – in spite of appearing to be merely sleeping. But then, we all do this to some extent. Scientists still don't fully understand the process of dreaming in adults, but the cycles of deep and REM (or rapid eye movement) sleep are patterns that your baby will have been getting used to even in the womb. What is certain is that these circadian rhythms – based on food, temperature and hormones – are pretty similar to ours and the shorter length of sleep is dictated by the baby's need to feed at regular intervals.

After about three months your baby should start sleeping for longer periods at night and have fewer daytime naps. Her sleep cycle will still be governed by the need for regular feeds, but at this stage you might be able to slowly establish a different 'day' and 'night' routine.

Day and night routines

Make sure that your baby gets plenty of stimulation during the day, and make daytime feeds as different as you can to those at night. Talk and sing, involve other members of the family, even have the telly on. If he falls asleep while feeding, gently wake him. And when he is daytime napping, don't be tempted to tiptoe round the house and make as little noise as you can. He'll be used to hearing the everyday sounds you make from before he was born, and in some cases he might even find them comforting.

By contrast, you should try and make things as calm and quiet before bedtime as you can. A routine of dimming lights, putting toys to bed before having a bath, a cuddle and a story can be a useful signal that this time he's expected to sleep for a little longer.

Worry

Babies are at their most vulnerable in these first few months of life, and one worry parents have is the risk of sudden infant death. After going through the physical and emotional roller coaster of pregnancy and birth and finally coming face-to-face with your baby you might think the worrying is over. But for many parents of newborns (not to mention children of all ages) the worry never stops. But the more you know and the more you do, the safer your baby will be.

Sudden Infant Death Syndrome (SIDS)

Sudden Infant Death Syndrome, sometimes known as cot death, is rare. In the first twelve months – when babies are at most risk – the rate is under 0.05%. But cot death is particularly frightening because so much about it is unknown. In spite of this, there are certain simple safeguards you can take to reduce the risk still further:

- Remember: 'back to sleep' and 'foot to feet' – place your baby on his back (and not the front or side) and with his feet at the bottom of the cot or cradle.

- Temperature – don't let your baby overheat and make sure his head is uncovered. Using a 'grow-bag' (baby sleeping bag) is a great way to make sure your baby doesn't get tangled up in sheets and blankets, for example.

- Keep the baby in the same room as you for the first six months, if possible.

- Avoid – or be especially careful if – co-sleeping. Babies can quickly overheat under a duvet or get tangled up in sheets, and a heavy adult in the bed can cause injury.

- Never sleep with your baby on a sofa or armchair.

- Never let anyone smoke in the same room as your baby.

For more information about SIDS, go to the Foundation for the Study of Infant Deaths' (FSIDS) website: http://fsid.org.uk/

Summing Up

- Don't be afraid to say 'no' to visitors.

- Don't be afraid to say 'yes' either. But don't fret about whether your clothes are ironed or if the vacuuming has been done. It's the baby they've come to see.

- Expect to be tired; sleep when you can (while the baby sleeps, for instance).

- Your partner needs you. Put her and the baby first.

- Don't worry if you don't get the attention that you're used to.

- Talk to other mums and dads. Don't be afraid to ask for advice.

Chapter Five

Three to Six Months Old

By now you'll be getting used to how much your life has changed. You may have established a routine and things will perhaps be settling down. You never know, you might even be getting a bit more sleep than you were in the first few days and months. But don't bank on it! During the next three months all sorts of things will be happening: by the age of six months most babies can imitate sounds, blow bubbles and sit up without being supported. They also weigh twice as much as they did at birth. The pace of change is quickening.

Your partner

Your partner will by now be slowly recovering from some of the physical effects of giving birth. But this process may be taking longer than usual, and some things may not return to normal. Stretch marks, for example, will almost certainly fade but may never disappear. And the muscles around your partner's bladder, anus and vagina may still be weakened.

Pelvic floor exercise

When you consider what happened 'down there' just a few short months ago, it isn't any wonder that the muscles of the pelvic area may need toning. Your partner was probably taught how to do pelvic floor exercises at the antenatal classes you attended. In fact, strengthening these muscles before giving birth can speed up the healing process afterwards. Basically, your partner needs to imagine that she's either stopping a bowel movement or stopping a wee. Doing this repeatedly – both quickly and then again more slowly – will gradually tone up the muscles and make it less likely that your partner will be troubled by any 'leakage'.

Stomach exercises

Restoring your partner's tummy to its pre-pregnancy shape is something she can help achieve by doing stomach muscle exercises like the ones outlined below. And without taking the role of her personal trainer, you could gently encourage your partner by running through the procedure a few times with her and helping her.

- First, your partner should lie on her side with her knees bent.
- Next, she should breathe in, while at the same time allowing her tummy muscles to relax.
- Then as she breathes out, she should slowly tuck the lower part of her tummy in and hold for a count of ten.
- Repeat this several times.

Another useful exercise for tummy muscles is similar to sit-ups, but less physically demanding:

- This time your partner should lie on her back with her knees bent.
- Then she should place one hand flat on her tummy and the other behind her head.
- As she breathes in, she should gently lift her head and shoulders off the floor as if she was attempting to do a sit-up.

But remember, doing a full sit-up at this stage is not a good idea.

Getting out and about

Getting a baby ready to go out can sometimes seem like a military operation. There's the clothing, the pushchair, the changing bag and possibly the next feed to consider. Sometimes it just seems easier to stay put.

Statistically, stay-at-home mums are more likely to be depressed than working mums. Part of the reason is that being at home with a baby can be very isolating. If your partner is at home for any length of time you'll need to encourage her to get out of the house and join some of the many playgroups, mother-and-toddler groups and other parent-child activity sessions that are out there.

If you're not sure where to begin, try your local Sure Start Centre. They'll usually offer a range of activities themselves, as well as having a variety of people to talk to. Sharing some of the highs and lows of coping with kids is a good way of relieving some of the stress. And looking after young children can be stressful. If your partner is doing this on her own, she might feel as if she's wading through treacle. Sometimes just doing a simple thing like putting a load of washing on can seem to take all day. Not only is that frustrating, but if your partner is used to getting things done efficiently at work or in the home it can lead to a build-up of stress and resentment.

Playgroups

Regardless of who is looking after the little one full-time, it's worth getting to grips with what the local community has to offer by way of 'mother' (not to mention father) and toddler groups, playgroups, nurseries etc. Many excellent sessions are run by voluntary groups in church and village halls. They can be a great way to get out and meet other people as well as being good for the baby.

Relationships

Both you and your partner might notice a change in your relationship following the birth of your child. Not only will this be due to obvious things like tiredness and hormones, but if you've returned to work and resumed your pre-child day-to-day life your partner might feel resentful and left out. It goes without saying that you should do your best to ease the burden, but understanding that your partner's feelings are a normal reaction to her situation is immensely important.

You

Being a dad isn't necessarily something that comes naturally and the role of the father has changed quite dramatically in recent years. Not long ago dads wouldn't have gone anywhere near the birth, never mind a dirty nappy. According to the National Childbirth Trust (NCT), over 95% of fathers are now present at the birth, compared to less than half that number in 1980.

'Encourage her to get out of the house and join some of the many playgroups, mother-and-toddler groups and other parent-child activity sessions that are out there.'

Research done recently by DadSpace (http://www.dads-space.com/) revealed that 57% of dads think they should be spending more time with their children, but that their working day makes it impossible. And almost 60% got home too late during the week to even give their kids a bath. It also revealed that British dads don't feel as confident (48%) or appreciated (43%) as mums; that the majority of dads surveyed (8 out of 10) agreed there wasn't enough information and support available for them, claiming they don't feel as confident as their partner or wife – particularly when it came to opening up and talking one-to-one with their children (41%); 26% of dads said their partner or wife took most of the parental responsibility.

The same survey also asked dads what they would do with their children if they had more time. And the things dads would like to do more of include:

- Playing their favourite sports with them (46%).
- Doing more after school activities (39%).
- Reading them their favourite bedtime story (40%).

The precious years of babyhood and early infancy pass so quickly. It might not seem like it after yet another sleepless night, but the day will come when you'll wonder where the time has gone.

Case study

'I have stayed at home to look after our daughter, while my wife has gone back to work. This has meant me not exactly giving up my career, but certainly putting it on hold for a while, and I suppose I am a bit jealous of my wife being able to go out and carry on working, especially on wet days when I'm stuck in the house with the little one. Of course, she's probably a lot more jealous of me, and one of the tensions has been that our daughter's first word was 'dada' and she constantly uses it when my wife's trying to play with her. I think it's made her even more determined to be the one to stay at home when we have another child in the future. I say 'when' rather than 'if' which clearly shows the whole experience hasn't put us off too much!'

Richard, father to Gwendolen, 12 months

Be there . . .

If possible, try to be present when your child has one of his or her routine check-ups at the clinic. Babies at this stage are routinely weighed and measured, then at six months there is a more thorough medical check-up (see 'Your baby' below). It's useful for both parents to be present if at all possible, both for practical reasons and as a sign of your involvement. Remember, you've a legal right to ask for some flexibility from your employer (see chapter 8 for details).

Your relationship

You're both tired, your baby and your partner will probably get all the attention and there may be occasions when you feel, well – left out. It can be quite difficult to get used to how much your life has changed and how little attention your partner has now got for you. As author and father-of-two Ben Wakeling says, 'You may feel isolated or frustrated from time to time, but it's to be expected as the focus in your relationship has shifted. Just roll with the punches – and, when your partner blames *you* for every little twinge, ache or pain, just take it on the chin!'

Your baby

Ready, steady . . .

On your marks for what is potentially the most exciting, fast-paced period of change in your new bundle of joy's short existence. From the age of three to six months children develop and grow at a rapid rate. At four months, for example, your baby should have developed neck muscles strong enough to be able to support the weight of her own head. She may also be able to support the weight of her body on her own legs but she won't be able to stand unaided, and you should avoid supporting her in a standing position for too long. Babies' bones aren't as hard as ours and can be damaged by excess strain. Babies also have more bones than adults – some 360 compared to an adult's average of 206 and at first, the toes don't have bones in them at all. It takes several months for the cartilage-like structures at the end of each foot to calcify into the genuine article, so be careful!

'It invariably has affected our relationship – a lot less of our attention and focus is on each other now – but we still find time to concentrate on our own relationship; "date nights", and the like.'

Ben Wakeling, parenting author

Developmental Milestones

Here are a few of the major developmental milestones to expect in the next three months:

- Holding up her head.
- Standing (bearing her own weight on her legs) whilst being supported or whilst holding on to something.
- Crawling, or bottom-shuffling.
- Rolling over, reaching out for things and grasping them or even pulling them towards her.
- Playing with her hands and feet.
- Recognising the sound of her own name.
- Imitating some of the sounds she hears and responding to the sound of your voice.
- Sitting up without support.

But remember, babies don't perform to expectations, and you may find yours doesn't show the slightest sign of doing something on that list or that she has already ticked off several items. Like people, they're all different. Because, of course, they are people and that fact is never more apparent than in the three to six months stage when aspects of an individual personality will start to emerge.

Weaning

Towards the age of six months you will probably find that your baby is ready to start eating solid foods. There's an awful lot written and said about weaning and advice seems to change from one year to the next. At the moment, official guidance suggests that six months is the right time to start a child on solids; just a few years ago and the same advice was to begin at four months.

What is certain is that your child will probably tell you when she's ready. Of course, she'll do it in her own way. Don't expect her to present you with an order for a three-course gourmet meal. But you may find that she seems less satisfied with milk, shows an interest in what you and the rest of the family are eating and seems to take an interest in chewing almost anything she can get her hands on. In fact, two of the most important readiness factors should also be present by the time you start to think about weaning: teeth, and the ability to sit up in a high chair.

Current medical advice is not to introduce cow's milk until your child is at least twelve months old and to avoid honey completely in the first year.

Teething

On average, babies tend to cut their first teeth around the six-month mark, although it varies enormously. Some are born with at least one tooth, whilst others might go a year or more without a single molar or incisor. What is certain is that whenever your baby starts teething, you'll know about it. Not necessarily because it's painful, but because there'll suddenly be bucketfuls of saliva dribbling down her chin. Other signs you might see are flushed cheeks and red or white patches on the gums themselves. By the time the whole thing is finished – at around two and a half – your baby should have a total of 20 primary teeth, evenly distributed top and bottom.

'Whenever your baby starts teething, you'll know about it.'

Illness

Understandably, babies succumb to all the common ailments, such as a cold, that afflict adults and older children. Their immune systems are only just kicking into action and for the first time they find themselves exposed to a world of germs and other nasties. Parents can do a lot to help, by simple hygiene measures, for example. If your baby is formula-fed make sure all the equipment is properly sterilised before you begin. And wash your hands before making up the feed.

Of course, breastfeeding – even if just for the first six weeks – will greatly increase your baby's chances of fighting off infections as the breast milk contains many of the mother's antibodies. This sort-of 'plugs in' your baby to its mum's immune system, rather than having to start the whole thing off from scratch which is the kind of head start your child would be very grateful for if it could tell you!

But in spite of everything, babies still get sick. Colds are a common problem in the first year and there's not a great deal you can do, apart from keeping your little one warm and giving her plenty of fluids. If your baby has a high temperature or if you're worried for any reason, see your doctor – most GPs will see babies and young children at short notice.

The six-month check-up

At around six months old, your baby will be given what's called a developmental review. The GP and health visitor will measure and record things like growth, eyesight and hearing, as well as watching her or asking you to check if she can do things like sit upright, roll over and perhaps crawl and reach for toys.

Play

Although in the first few weeks and months it can sometimes seem as though life for your baby is all eating, sleeping, feeding and crying; there will be times when none of this is happening and you might wonder what to do.

A mat on the floor for your baby to lie and kick his legs, some soft toys to see and hold, a bouncing chair, a mobile or a baby gym are all great ways to stimulate your baby in those early days. Play hearing games by making noises (blowing raspberries seems to appeal to almost every baby) or shaking a rattle and seeing how your baby reacts to gentle music. Sing – anything – no matter how good or bad you think you are. Your baby might just be your most adoring audience.

Although a newborn's hearing is quite well developed, babies don't like loud noises so talk, sing or play music softly. Your baby's sight will take a longer time to develop, and she'll only be able to focus on objects about ten inches away at first. Not surprisingly, faces are a big attraction to a little baby. Playing peekaboo makes looking at your face into a game, and one that all babies seem to find amusing.

'By six months your baby will have doubled body weight compared to when it was born. By the end of the first year it will have doubled it again.'

Summing Up

- Although your partner will be slowly recovering from the birth, remember some things – like stretch marks – may not return to normal.

- Encourage your partner to do her pelvic floor exercises to make sure the muscles of the pelvic area return to normal.

- No matter how much time it seems to take getting a baby ready to go out, make sure you do. It'll be good for you all.

- Don't forget your relationship with your partner will have changed forever. Be understanding, help as much as possible and make sure the change is for the better.

Chapter Six

Six to Twelve Months Old

By now you'll have established a routine (of sorts) and feel that you're old hands at the parenting game. Unfortunately, someone keeps on moving the goalposts and the game keeps changing. No sooner have you got used to looking after a tiny baby then they're not a tiny baby anymore. That helpless little bundle you were cradling so gently just six months ago can now move around and make a range of noises; he can smile and laugh and not just cry, and hopefully he's got the message that the night-time is for sleeping. Maybe!

Your partner

Sex

While there are some women who will want sex almost as soon as the birth is over, you'll probably find that it can take time to recover, physically and mentally, before your partner is ready for sex again. As one mum from Manchester told me, it was only 'when the headache/stitches/tiredness excuses were too old!' that she and her partner started to think seriously about it. And when they did (after a couple of months) it wasn't quite what either of them had expected. If the birth has been difficult and there has been tearing or your partner had an episiotomy then it could take a while before she feels comfortable having sex. Or rather, penetrative sex. Don't forget there are any number of ways for you and your partner to share sexual intimacy without necessarily going there!

'That helpless little bundle you were cradling so gently just six months ago can now move around and make a range of noises.'

Breastfeeding

If your partner is fully breastfeeding there'll still be plenty of pregnancy hormones swimming around her body. That means that if you do have sex, she's highly unlikely to become pregnant. Just as you can't get pregnant 'again' once you already are, these hormones prevent ovulation and act as a natural form of contraception. After all, your partner wouldn't want to be coping with early-pregnancy symptoms like morning sickness whilst looking after a toddler. But be careful – this method can't be relied on! And although some mums carry on breastfeeding after six months or even twelve, others find that – once weaning starts – the baby's need for breast milk diminishes. And lactation is a sensitive supply-and-demand phenomenon: once junior stops wanting, mummy stops (or starts to stop) producing. All of which is a rather roundabout way of saying that – if your partner doesn't want to immediately step back onto the treadmill of pregnancy – you'll need to think of using contraception.

Contraception

For a variety of reasons, resuming the oral contraceptive is not usually advised. Whilst the mini-pill is often fine, if your partner is breastfeeding the hormones contained in the full version can pass through the milk to the baby. Other reasons for avoiding the pill include complications that can occasionally occur post-birth, so it is as well to think of other methods if you and your partner aren't planning an immediate addition to your family.

You

As the weeks and months go by and some semblance of routine becomes established (if you're lucky!) you'll find that little DIY list will come back into its own. It's stereotypical, perhaps, and no doubt you'll have changed as many nappies as your partner, but it's often dads that get the job of making sure the home is safe for an increasingly mobile baby.

Child safety

Children learn in a variety of ways. They copy what they see but they also need to try things out for themselves and learn from experience. And as they become mobile you'll need to make sure the home remains a safe environment.

There are a number of things you'll need to do to make the home safe for your child, and you might as well start now. Before you know it crawling will have given way to walking, so:

- Ensure sharp corners on furniture are covered.

- Fit a fireguard, if you haven't done already.

- Make sure anything sharp or otherwise dangerous is well out of reach. This includes sharp knives at the edges of kitchen work surfaces. Once he can stand or pull himself up, it won't be long before he's reaching out for whatever he can grasp.

- Always make sure medicines and cleaning material are stored in a child-proof cabinet. You can buy small 'locks' which are really just child-proof catches for cupboard doors and drawers and they can be fitted within seconds.

- Stair safety gate. It won't be long before he attempts his first ascent of the north face of the staircase if you don't.

- Socket covers. All children seem to find electric sockets, with their tiny finger-sized holes and lovely clicking switches, fascinating. Simple, inexpensive plastic covers will make sure your child doesn't come to any harm as he explores.

'Studies have shown that a good early bond between a child and its father sets up the child for a future of successful relationships.'

Who's the daddy?

If some of my words are making you feel a little bit peripheral to your child's development, think again. Although the role of mums and dads is different – and let's face it, there are certain things dads can't do – more and more research is proving that dads matter, and matter enormously. The quality of a child's relationship with his or her father is every bit as important as that with the mother, and studies have shown that a good early bond between a child and its father sets up the child for a future of successful relationships.

Making time

All of which means, especially if you've gone back to work, that you'll have to make time to get it right. If you're at work and your partner is doing the lion's share of looking after the baby, make sure you take the opportunity to take over when you can. Some men feel helpless when a young child cries, for example, and hand the situation over to the mother. But there's nothing physical that says a man can't read the signs and act on the cues given. Learn from your partner, and learn together. Remember, your partner might have it slightly stronger, but – however mildly by comparison – your hormones are responding to the sound of the baby crying too. Your body is being told that the child needs some attention in a variety of ways, from a quickening of the pulse to mild perspiration. So don't fight it – go with it.

Get involved

There are any number of things a busy, full-time working dad can do to help, whether it's in the evenings or at weekends. I've already mentioned nappy-changing, bottle feeding, bathing and the like. But just by being there – enjoying the company of your children even if you're 'doing' something else – you're showing them you value the time you spend together.

And although it might be too early to get the train set out just yet, dads can still:

- Go to the park.
- Pull funny faces (we're good at that, so I've been told).
- Read a bedtime story.
- Sing songs.
- Smile, and of course,
- Talk

. . . to their children.

Your baby

Between six months and a year, babies also start to assert themselves and develop into little individuals with their own distinct personalities and habits. At first you might notice your baby beginning to take an interest in the world around them. They will begin to sit upright unaided, even if only for a short time and maybe start to move around. And now that your baby doesn't need his arms as much for support, you will almost certainly find him reaching out and grabbing things for himself. So be warned!

Developmental milestones

Although many of the really important changes that mark the end of babyhood and the beginning of childhood start to happen at this stage, the pace can vary enormously. For example, some babies can begin to hold and drink from a 'sippy' cup, understand language and begin to use words (especially their own name and the words 'yes' and 'no'). There will be 'early walkers' and 'early talkers' in this category too, but for some the pace of change will be slower. Generally, signs to look out for might include:

- The ability to anticipate (e.g. a parent coming home from work) as well as the strength to wave 'bye-bye'.

- A basic sense of himself and his environment (which can manifest as separation anxiety or a fear of strangers if you're not careful).

- Object permanence, or the ability to know that toys still exist even when they can't see them.

- An interest in other children.

- An increasing drive for independence.

Some of these changes occur quite naturally. Others need encouragement and careful nurturing. Talk to him and use his name; stimulate him as much as possible, but remember that his attention span will be no more than a few minutes long. In fact, the days of lying contented on his mat or in his baby gym for up to ten or fifteen minutes may be over, and you may find your baby becoming bored more quickly. So make sure there are interesting things for him to see and do and safe objects for him to pick up.

Eating and drinking

As mentioned in the previous chapter, six months is the time when most parents begin to introduce food other than milk into their child's diet. The current recommendation is for children to be exclusively fed on breast milk for the first six months of life, but this is the World Health Organisation's (WHO) advice based on what is considered best practice across the globe. Practically, parents might begin slowly introducing 'solids' a little earlier, but remember, although 'follow-on' milk (a richer, more nourishing version) is a practical solution for a hungry baby, cows' and goats' milk must be avoided (as should honey) entirely for the first twelve months.

'All babies are different, and develop at different speeds and the developmental "milestones" will never be the same for every child.'

When children begin eating solid food they will start to require more liquid in the form of drinks than before. Water straight from the mains supply can be safely given to a child over six months of age (before that it should be boiled, then allowed to cool) but take care if using bottled water as the mineral content might be unsuitable for small children. Similarly, tea and coffee should be avoided as they reduce iron absorption, as should all fizzy drinks and squashes. The most healthy option for a child over the age of six months is a citrus fruit juice (e.g. fresh orange) diluted and given in a cup at mealtimes. They're a great source of vitamin C, and giving them at mealtimes greatly helps it to be absorbed into the body.

Childhood illnesses

No matter how careful you are, your child is almost certainly going to fall ill at some stage. Indeed, don't be too fastidious about germs and cleanliness, as research suggests small amounts of exposure are actually good for the developing immune system. Children who grow up in an excessively sterile environment also seem to suffer more from allergies and severe reactions to environmental irritation.

Chickenpox

This is rare in very early infancy, but from the age of about one year upwards the chances of your child catching chickenpox are quite high. Indeed, some people have been known to hold 'chickenpox parties' for older children and although that's emphatically not recommended, the advantage of contracting this and other common childhood infections like mumps and measles in childhood is considerable, as complications can set in when caught as an adult.

So why is chickenpox so common in young children? Probably at least in part because the disease is infectious before the rash even appears (and thus before you know your child has got it) and can incubate for about a fortnight. It remains infectious until all the spots (red spots that blister before scabbing over) dry up. Your baby will start to feel unwell 14-16 days after catching it – see your doctor to confirm that it is chickenpox.

Chickenpox can cause serious complications for anyone who is, or is trying to become pregnant, so avoid all contact if you can.

Measles

Measles is a virus spread through airborne transmission and again is highly contagious. Although some cases can be relatively mild, it can lead to serious complications, including convulsions, brain inflammation and deafness. Early signs are usually a high temperature, coughing, runny nose and eyes and the characteristic measles 'rash' may only appear several days after these initial symptoms.

Mumps

Mumps is a viral infection which lasts for about seven to ten days and usually brings about painful swelling in the glands of the face, neck and jaw. In males it can also lead to swelling of the testes; women can also suffer swollen ovaries. Occasionally, mumps can lead to deafness and even to viral meningitis (swelling of the brain lining, or meninges).

'Always seek medical advice if you think your child is ill. Keep him as comfortable as possible and maintain his fluid intake. Consider infant paracetamol if your GP recommends it.'

See the doctor

As always with illnesses and children, seek medical advice and have a doctor confirm your diagnosis. Other than that the main thing to do is keep your child as comfortable as possible and help prevent them scratching the spots. Calamine lotion often helps reduce the itching in cases of chickenpox and measles, as does wearing comfortable, loose clothing to avoid rubbing. Maintain your child's fluid intake and consider infant paracetamol if your GP recommends it.

Immunisations

'Although some people think that childhood vaccinations carry risks, experts think that the dangers arising from the infections far outweigh any minor risks arising from the vaccination.'

Between 12 and 15 months you will be offered a vaccination for measles, mumps and rubella (MMR). This is often offered as a combined three-in-one vaccine, although a while ago there was some concern about its safety and a few parents either declined to have their children vaccinated or opted for each vaccine to be administered separately. This is obviously only something that you and your partner can decide, but expert advice is that the risk of complications from any of these three infections far outweighs any minor risks arising from the vaccination.

A list of the recommended schedule for childhood immunisations is given below:

2 months:

- Diphtheria, tetanus, pertussis (whooping cough), polio and Haemophilus influenzae type b (Hib, a bacterial infection that can cause severe pneumonia or meningitis in young children) given as a 5-in-1 single jab known as DTaP/IPV/Hib.

- Pneumococcal infection.

3 months:

- 5-in-1, second dose (DTaP/IPV/Hib).

- Meningitis C.

4 months:

- 5-in-1, third dose (DTaP/IPV/Hib).

- Pneumococcal infection, second dose.

- Meningitis C, second dose.

Between 12 and 13 months:

- Meningitis C, third dose.

- Hib, fourth dose (Hib/MenC given as a single jab).

- MMR (measles, mumps and rubella), given as a single jab.

- Pneumococcal infection, third dose.

3 years and 4 months, or soon after:

- MMR second jab.

- Diphtheria, tetanus, pertussis and polio (DtaP/IPV), given as a 4-in-1 pre-school booster.

(Source: NHS Direct)

Summing Up

- As your child becomes more mobile, you'll need to make sure your home is a safe environment for him/her as they start to explore.

- If you're back at work, try and take the opportunity to take over from your partner when you can. She'll need a break.

- At six months many parents begin to introduce food other than milk into their child's diet, but cows' and goats' milk must be avoided (as should honey) entirely for the first twelve months.

- When your child starts eating solid food they'll start to drink more than before. Water straight from the mains supply is fine, but avoid bottled water and sweet drinks.

- Remember, all babies are different and develop at different speeds. The development milestones are only guidelines, but if you're worried about your child's progress ask your GP or health visitor.

Chapter Seven

One Year to Three Years Old

This chapter covers a relatively large period of time. At the start your child might still seem like a baby; by the end he or she won't be a toddler but will almost certainly be walking and talking with confidence.

Your partner

A normal life

If your partner isn't breastfeeding, she might find that her menstrual cycle begins to return to normal as early as the fourth month (or sometimes even earlier). This means that you will both need to start thinking again about contraception – or at least that you will if you don't plan to have more children at the moment. That assumes, of course, that your partner is ready to start enjoying sex again – which in turn depends on how well she's recovered after giving birth. You might find you want to get back into the swing of things rather sooner than your partner. Understand that this is not always possible. Quite apart from her physical recovery, it may take time for your partner to feel ready for sex. And, of course, you might just find that you're both too tired!

Returning to work

If your partner is returning to work, you will need to consider who is going to look after the baby and what needs to be done in terms of practicalities like breastfeeding. In addition, there will inevitably be some soul-searching. Most people assume that working parents spend less time with their offspring than used to be the case. But for a variety of reasons, modern working parents might actually end up spending *more* time with their children than was normal forty or fifty years ago.

- A host of labour-saving devices means whoever runs the home doesn't have to spend all day in the kitchen.

- Dads who work typically don't spend as much time in the pub – or out of the house – now as they used to.

- Mums probably see more of their children because, as a rule, kids don't play out as much as they once did. Days of leaving home after breakfast and returning when you were hungry like we used to (in the 'good old days') tend not to happen.

Childcare

A variety of childcare options exist and these are discussed in detail in chapter 8. Choosing the best for you will depend on factors like the hours worked as well as the needs of your baby. There is more detail both on the options available and the help you might be entitled to in the final chapter. For now, if your partner is planning to return to work it will be important to consider:

- What care best suits the needs both of your child and yours and your partner's working hours. Some nurseries and pre-schools, for example, only work school hours which might make it difficult if you or your partner are unable to leave work in time.

- If your child is used to spending time alone with you or your partner, a local childminder might be a better option than a busy nursery. But that will depend, of course, on what is available in your area.

'Most people assume that working parents spend less time with their offspring than used to be the case. But for a variety of reasons, modern working parents might actually end up spending *more* time with their children.'

Expressing milk

If breastfeeding, your partner will need to be able to express milk at work and refrigerate it for later use. This means that whoever looks after the baby in your partner's absence will still be able to feed him using a bottle. She'll need a breast pump and a supply of bottles or bags. Her employer may need to provide a refrigerator to store the milk, as well as somewhere private for her to express during the day.

You

By now your baby (who is really a baby no longer) will be showing increasingly strong traits of individual personality. The process of learning what is and isn't acceptable behaviour is a complex one, and discipline is often seen as a dad's duty. The fact is you should both assume responsibility for teaching your child right from wrong. And above all, you should agree on where the lines are to be drawn and what sanctions you'll impose very early on. It's not true that young children are manipulative little mini-Machiavellis, constantly scheming to see if they can find a weakness in their parents' resolve. But saying something that's different to your partner is, quite simply, confusing. You need to be giving clear, consistent and – above all – fair rules for them to follow. And one of the most important rules of all isn't for them at all – it's for the parents.

Do as you would be done by

Children are, above all, simple creatures. They crave consistency, and they learn most powerfully from what they see and hear around them. You and your partner should therefore always try to model the behaviour you want your child to follow. If you want him to say 'please' and 'thank you' make sure you do too – both to him and anyone else when he might be listening. Humans have evolved by learning quickly from what they see and hear around them. No matter how many times you tell them to do something, if they don't see you doing it children will learn pretty soon that it's not important and forget about it.

'It's not true that young children are manipulative little mini-Machiavellis, constantly scheming to see if they can find a weakness in their parents' resolve.'

The road to school

When children reach the age of three, they qualify for some free pre-school education. This can take a variety of forms and adds up to several hours per week. If your child already attends a pre-school, childminder or day nursery you may well be able to use this entitlement to offset some of the cost. There is more information on the financial help available to parents at the end of this book. But it won't be that much longer before you'll have to start to consider formal schooling, and this is the subject of the next section.

Starting school

I know. And in a section headed 'One to Three Years Old' too. But let's face it. Your baby isn't a baby anymore. And sooner or later you're going to have to start thinking about the dreaded 'S' word. And when you do, a little information can help take you a long way.

There's a lot of confusion about schooling in the UK, not least of which is the misapprehension that it's compulsory. Going to school isn't; ensuring your child has a proper education is. Some people do it at home, with great success. But the vast majority of us choose to put our trust in the professionals. And that means getting your name down for a school by the time your child is three.

School-starting ages vary across the UK, as do admission procedures. Most primary schools now admit children into a Reception class when they are four years old, so you need to start planning ahead and thinking about which school you'd like your child to attend by the time they're three.

Good schools are often over-subscribed, and they'll have policies for deciding who gets a place if there aren't enough to meet demand. For state schools (non fee-paying) procedures are overseen by the Local Education Authority (LEA) although if the school has Foundation or Voluntary Aided status its own governing body will decide the criteria for themselves. By law no state school can use an interview as part of its selection procedure, and the most common factors usually include:

- Distance from the school.

- A brother or sister already at the school.

- Attendance at a church or other place of worship (if the school is a faith school).

Independent schools – and some state secondary schools – can select all or some of their intake on the basis of general academic ability (often assessed by means of an entrance exam) or aptitude for a particular curriculum area.

The first day

Although it's technically beyond the scope of this chapter and lies a year or more into the future, it's worth considering what you can do to make your child's first days at school as straightforward as possible. Here are just a few things that will help the transition go smoothly:

- Visit the school with your son or daughter beforehand. Talk to the class teacher. Find out as much as you can about that important first day.

- Get your child used to the routine of getting up and getting ready, so that the first school run isn't a problem.

- Speak to other parents, including those with kids already at the school. No matter how much official information you receive, there'll always be something they can tell you that will make a difference.

For more information on what to do and what to expect when your child starts primary school, have a look at *Primary School – A Parent's Guide* (Need2Know).

Your baby

I suppose the first thing to say is that your baby is hardly your baby anymore. And if you think things have changed rapidly in the first twelve months, prepare yourself for a shock. The pace of change quickens and – during this period – your child will start to walk, talk, eat proper food and do a host of other exciting and challenging things.

At the beginning of the time dealt with in this chapter he/she will almost certainly be crawling, may have started walking and might soon have started talking. By the end, he'll probably be running (rings around his parents if you're not too careful!) talking ten to the dozen and learning faster than at any other time in his short history. In short, your baby is growing up fast, and is now on the threshold of toddlerdom!

The developing child

As he or she grows up, the range and level of stimulation required will increase considerably. Blowing raspberries on your little darling's tummy might still be among the most amusing games for you both to play, but your son or daughter will need to be engaged in a variety of physical and intellectually challenging activities as he or she moves from age one to three.

Food and drink

'If you think things have changed rapidly in the first twelve months, prepare yourself for a shock.'

After the first year of a baby's life when he's typically half as long again and weighs three times what he did at birth, your baby's appetite might start to tail off. This is perfectly normal. As long as your child is eating and drinking healthily and regularly there'll be little need to worry or – worse – start making mealtimes a battleground. But your child's diet needs to be as healthy as you can make it. Variety isn't just the spice of life, it's the secret of a healthy diet for the whole family. Try to include something from each of the following four food groups on a regular basis:

- Dairy – milk (obviously) and that can include cow's milk from the age of one year. This should be full fat and not skimmed (semi-skimmed is acceptable from the age of two) as children need the extra fat and vitamins it contains. Also cheese, yoghurt, fromage frais, and eggs (fully cooked, as young children are more susceptible to food poisoning than adults).

- Fresh fruit and vegetables – most children can be persuaded to eat at least something from the range of fruit and veg available, but remember their taste buds are much more sensitive and 'forcing' them to eat something that they really do not like is counter-productive. Try 'disguising' it by mixing vegetables as the ingredients of a dish that you've prepared for the whole family, or make eating them a game.

- Bread, cereal and potatoes – including rice and pasta. Eat wholegrain varieties if possible, as they contain the nutrients from all three parts of the grain but don't add extra bran as this can interfere with the absorption of iron.

- Meat and fish – choose lean meat and try to include oily fish at least once per week. Alternatives to meat include beans, lentils, nuts etc.

Children have small stomachs and can't eat large meals all in one go, so snacking is also important. Make sure they, too, are as healthy as possible.

Other children

Until the age of about four, most children don't really interact with their peers: older siblings, adults and so on are more likely companions in the sense that we normally understand the word. Playing with other children, joining in games and becoming 'social' in the traditional sense is something that develops naturally from about the age of three onwards and an important learning stage for this is the playful interaction a child has with her parents. That means you.

As they grow older though, children naturally begin to take interest in the activities of each other. Learning to share, to control aggression, frustration and anger are all useful lessons to be learned from this early interaction with other children.

Siblings

It's likely to be during the period when your child is aged between one and three years that you and your partner may start thinking about adding to your family – especially if the baby was your first. If so, there is probably some basic advice worth considering now, as the process of preparing an existing child or children for the arrival of a sibling has to take place long before the new brother or sister arrives.

- As hard as it might seem, try not to make comparisons.
- Expect them to be different.

- Expect some sibling-rivalry: it's normal, especially if the age gap is greater than two years.

- Be prepared to work twice as hard!

Speech and language

Language skills are among the most important things that children develop during this period. Your child's first words will gradually become clearer and will be placed in ever more complicated phrases. By the time he's three, whole sentences will almost certainly be common and the sound of words might be accompanied by a curiosity to find out what they look like, especially when bedtime stories are being read.

Whilst children develop at different rates and – to an extent – are all going to be different, some stages in development are crucial. Evidence suggests that if children miss out then learning or acquiring key skills – like the ability to talk – might be more difficult or even impossible later on. Speech is a good example; it seems that unless a child is given systematic exposure to language by the age of seven, he or she will find it difficult or impossible to learn to speak in later life.

Some parents worry about 'teaching' language skills (other than speech) to their children, believing that they might do some harm if they approach it in the wrong way and the child is taught something different when he starts school. In reality, the more you do to familiarise your child with numbers, words, letters, sounds and concepts at this pre-school stage the better. You'll find a child of three can easily recognise their own name with a little help. And even if it doesn't lead to tangible progress, the interest you and your partner show in your growing child's learning will be the single biggest factor in his future educational success. A lot of people worry about choosing the right school, and teachers and formal learning are – of course – vitally important. But it's what parents do at home, in many cases merely by showing an active interest in their children's educational development, which makes the biggest difference.

'Your child's first words will gradually become clearer and will be placed in ever more complicated phrases.'

Walking

Many toddlers are doing just that – toddling – from about the age of one year onwards. Although the transition from this to what can truthfully be called 'walking' may take much longer and – as ever – children are different. If yours hasn't started yet, don't worry. Whilst most children crawl before they walk, some don't; some take longer than others for all sorts of reasons and while some stages are crucial to the ability of children to develop normally, there's no evidence to suggest that late walkers (or talkers, for that matter) are at any disadvantage. As ever, if you're worried talk to your GP or health visitor.

But when they do, it opens up a whole new world of home safety – a young child, newly mobile, combined with heaps of natural curiosity could be a recipe for disaster. So if you haven't done so yet, make sure:

- All harmful substances, like bleach, are out of sight and out of reach. This includes cleaning materials, medicines, knives and other sharp objects. Remember, now he's walking he'll be able to reach twice as far.

- Drawer safety catches. Investigating the cutlery drawer while you've got your back turned in the kitchen is a wonderfully amusing game – until disaster strikes.

- Dishwasher – always close the door, and ensure (whatever the manufacturer's instructions say) that knives are pointing down in the cutlery tray.

Potty-training

At some point during the first three years you no doubt start to think of potty-training. Chances are somebody you'll know will have done it with their child months ago and tell you that it only took a couple of weeks. In fact, Gina Ford says it can take as little as a week. And, if we're talking about getting your child used to the routine of using a potty, I suppose it can. But avoid either feeling pressurised to do it quickly, or to meet a spurious deadline. Children develop individually; your son or daughter will be ready when he or she is ready; indeed, starting it too early can and does lead to having to abandon it completely and return to it much later.

The key points to remember are:

- Few children are able to control their bowel and bladder before about 18 months; starting earlier sometimes works, but for the majority of children successful potty-training will occur between 18 and 24 months.

- If you notice that your child's nappy is dry (say, after a nap) it might be a sign that he or she is beginning to exert some control over their bodily functions. Similarly if he goes quiet or – more commonly – hides or takes himself off to another room when doing a poo, it shows an awareness of what is happening that can be the basis of successful potty-training.

- You and your partner must have the time to devote to the task. In reality, this is probably the most important factor in the entire enterprise. The message that the potty and/or lavatory (complete with child-sized loo seat) is now the place to do your business is quickly learned, but easily forgotten. Making an effort one day and not bothering the next is just confusing, and probably the biggest cause of potty-training failures. If you haven't got the time to go for it consistently for about a fortnight, it's probably not the right time to start.

'Bath time usually becomes more fun as children grow older.'

Bath time

Although you'll probably be an old-hand at it by now, bath time usually becomes more fun as children grow older. Although it's still probably not necessary to bath your child more than three or four times a week, if he or she enjoys splashing about in the water then it's easy to make it a nightly ritual if only to begin the 'wind down' to bedtime. And whatever division of labour you and your partner decide upon, bath time is often the sole preserve of dads. It's important to use only the mildest soaps, shampoos and other additives, as a child's skin is still very sensitive. Although bubble bath is fun, some can be heavily-scented and unsuitable for a young child's skin, so make sure you buy something that's family-friendly. And there's nothing wrong with a bath in good old clear water, either.

Bath toys – from the essential rubber duck to a flotilla of small ships – can be good fun, too. But you don't need to spend any money if you don't want to. Children will be just as happy with an empty plastic bottle! Just make sure that nothing you use is a choking hazard, as at this stage – whatever the state of the water – everything is likely to go into the mouth.

Head lice

Nasty little critters these, and it's unlikely that you'll get away without at least one dose of the dreaded 'nits' unless you decamp to a remote island and live with your brood in total isolation. Children are naturally sociable creatures, and getting up close and personal with one another is the perfect way for *Pediculus humanus capiti* to spread. The good news – yes, there is some good news – is that human head lice (unlike body lice, for instance) don't carry other diseases. So all you've got to contend with is itching, biting, scratching and possible widespread family infestation.

What to do

First, adopt a Corporal Jones approach: don't panic. They won't cause lasting harm, having them is almost a rite of passage and it doesn't reflect in any way on your family's personal hygiene. (It's a fact that lice prefer to live on clean heads!) Next, inform your child's nursery or childminder, playground, friends and parents etc. Next, check your own and other family members' heads for lice. It's highly likely that they've spread. Look at your pillow for anything that looks like fine pepper (but don't collect it up and use it to season your dinner – these are lice droppings!) and wash your bedding immediately.

'Adopt a Corporal Jones approach: don't panic.'

Treatments

Get thee a louse comb! Before you even consider treatment, you need to be sure what you think is there is there. A fine-toothed louse comb is probably the best way of establishing whether or not your child has nits. With the hair wet (bath time is a good time for louse-hunting) part and comb repeatedly, looking for telltale grey or brown specks. Putting something like a bowl under your child's head may help, as they'll almost certainly fall from the hair as you comb. In fact, many people insist this is the best way to get rid of them. Lice shampoos are certainly not thought worth the money, so the only other way of treating them effectively is by using an insecticide on your child's scalp. But you should go to your local pharmacy, rather than the garden centre. And beware: some lotions can only be had on prescription, and others may be unsuitable to use if your partner is pregnant.

Immunisations

Finally, a note about what to expect by way of immunisations at this stage. A booster injection for diphtheria and tetanus, plus an oral booster of the polio vaccine is usually given between the ages of three and five years. For a full list of the recommended schedule of vaccinations, see chapter 6.

Summing Up

◾ This stage is one of the most dramatic: a one-year-old is still a baby, but by the age of three he or she won't even be a toddler but will almost certainly be walking and talking with confidence.

◾ Don't assume you've got to be giving your child wall-to-wall, active attention 24/7. Sometimes just being in the same room, enjoying the same space, is enough.

◾ If your partner is returning to work, you will need to consider who is going to look after your child and what needs to be done in terms of practicalities, like breastfeeding.

Chapter Eight

Financial Help and Legal Entitlements

There is a whole raft of benefits and payments available both to expectant mothers and existing parents. Some are universal (which means they're available to everyone, regardless of income); others might be means-tested, meaning that you qualify for help if your income makes it likely that you'll need it.

In pregnancy

All pregnant women qualify for free dental care and free NHS prescriptions, both while they are pregnant and for several months after the birth of their child. This is because of the greater likelihood of them needing medical help at some point. For example, pregnant women are thought to be at greater risk of dental conditions like gingivitis (swollen and bleeding gums) during pregnancy, while the calcium needed to support the growth of an unborn baby can lead to the mother's own reserves being depleted.

Child Benefit

At present, every child up to the age of eighteen (provided they're in full-time education) qualifies for Child Benefit, regardless of household income. It's one of the many benefits of the welfare state, paid for out of National Insurance contributions and general taxation. Although everyone qualifies, not everyone claims it and yet doing so couldn't be easier.

Making a claim

If you or your partner is thinking of staying at home to look after your child, it's important that whichever of you gives up work (or reduces their hours) claims Child Benefit in their name. This is because Child Benefit carries with it an additional entitlement called 'Home Responsibilities Protection'. If you give up work completely, or reduce your hours significantly to look after your child you will probably find that you don't end up paying National Insurance contributions. This will affect your state pension entitlement. But for each year in which you don't work (or don't work enough to pay the full stamp) you'll be credited with full National Insurance contributions, protecting the level of your state pension. This means your claim for Child Benefit should be made in the name of the child's main carer, which makes perfect sense anyway.

'If you think you qualify, apply quickly as credits can only be backdated for three months.'

Child Tax Credit

Child Tax Credit is a form of tax relief paid by the government directly to working parents. Between them, couples with children must be working for a minimum of 24 hours per week and be earning less than £55,000 per year. Remember, this is your combined household income, and includes what both you and your partner earn together with any benefits you receive. Child Tax Credit is paid in addition to (and not affected by) Child Benefit payments, and can be paid either weekly into the bank or building society account of the parent making the claim, or every four weeks. If you think you qualify, apply quickly as credits can only be backdated for three months. To see if you are eligible for Child Tax Credit, contact HM Revenue & Customs and ask for a claim pack. And if your circumstances change (e.g. you get a pay rise) don't forget to let HM Revenue & Customs know.

Working Tax Credit

If you're in work but on a low wage you might also qualify for Working Tax Credit. In addition, parents claiming Working Tax Credit might be entitled to help towards the costs of childcare. As before, it depends on the number of hours worked and the level of your joint household income and you need to contact your local HM Revenue & Customs office to find out if you qualify, and how to claim.

Need2Know

Job Grant

Job Grant is a tax-free lump sum you may also be entitled to, especially if you're returning to work after a period of unemployment or unpaid childcare. It is paid when you begin full-time work for a minimum of 16 hours a week. You'll get it if you (and your partner, if you have one) are aged 25 or over and you've been getting one or more of these benefits for at least 26 weeks before you started work:

* Income Support.
* Jobseeker's Allowance (both types).
* Incapacity Benefit.
* Severe Disablement Allowance.

For parents the grant is £250.

At the time of writing, the government has proposed a gradual change to the benefit system, replacing many of the individual benefits listed above (along with others such as Disability Living Allowance) with a single Universal Credit. This change is being introduced slowly and won't fully be in place until at least 2015.

Child Maintenance

If you're faced with the prospect of bringing up a child alone, you may need to apply for some form of child maintenance. This is paid by the non-resident parent, and since April 2010 it has been possible for all lone parents – whether or not they are in receipt of other financial benefits (e.g. Jobseeker's Allowance) – to make arrangements themselves with their partner rather than apply through the Child Support Agency. And your entitlement to benefits is not affected by receiving child maintenance from a former partner in this way.

'If you're bringing up a child alone, don't forget you may be able to apply for some form of child maintenance to be paid by the absent parent.'

Child Support Agency

If arranging matters between yourselves is difficult, you can ask the Child Support Agency (CSA) for help in establishing regular child maintenance payments. This is a free service, and arrangements made through the CSA are legally binding. This means that if a partner fails to help pay for the upkeep of his or her child, they can be taken to court and the payments taken direct from his or her salary. If tracing an absent parent is a problem, or if obtaining personal financial information is difficult, the CSA can go direct to an employer or the government in an effort to get the information needed for a settlement. Once the CSA has made an arrangement, you are legally obliged to follow its decision.

Childcare

Working parents are entitled to two distinct forms of help with the costs of childcare:

- Nursery vouchers
- Childcare vouchers

Although in practice these two entitlements may overlap and they sound almost identical, they are different and administered in completely different ways. It's important that you understand them and know how and when to apply for them.

Nursery Vouchers

From the age of three, all children in England are entitled to a minimum 15 hours of free pre-school education per week for 38 weeks of the year. This can take place in nurseries, playgroups, pre-schools or with a registered childminder. The benefit is universal (meaning it applies to everyone regardless of their income) and not means-tested.

When your child qualifies for a free place:

- If your child is born between 1st April and 31st August he or she will be eligible for a free place from 1st September following their third birthday until statutory school age

- If your child is born between 1st September and 31st December he or she will be eligible for a free place from 1st January following their third birthday until statutory school age

- Or, if born between 1st January and 31st March the free entitlement starts on 1st April following their third birthday until statutory school age.

This is a free, universal entitlement (meaning it applies to everyone, regardless of income) but it may not cover your family's needs because of things like work commitments. If this is the case you may be able to get further financial help with the costs of extra childcare.

Childcare vouchers

In addition, there are things called childcare vouchers which you can buy through your employer in order to help offset the costs. These vouchers are paid out of your pre-tax salary, which is called a 'salary sacrifice'. This means that they end up being worth more to you than the money you hand over in order to get them, the difference being the tax you would have paid if you'd taken the cost as part of your salary. In cash terms, parents paying the basic 20% rate of tax can buy vouchers worth a total of £55 per week (£243 per month). Of course, you can only use them to offset the cost of childcare. But don't forget you are paying it out of what is in effect untaxed income, so for a basic-rate taxpayer it's worth an extra 20% in real terms.

Not all employers take part in this scheme, so approach your employer to find out if this is an option for you and/or your partner. Some employers allow you to backdate the vouchers for up to six months and they have a long expiry date. And you can apply for them as soon as your child is born.

Childcare vouchers can be used to help pay for the costs of childcare for all children up to the age of 15 and the benefit is available to each working parent (so if both you and your partner work, you can both buy up to £55 worth of vouchers per week). And they're not specific to a particular child: you can 'mix and match' your use of these vouchers with all your children.

Different childcare options

Of course, it's all very well claiming such benefits and making sure you get the most out of the available support, but finding the right childcare provider for your son or daughter is something you and your partner will want to consider very carefully. From nursery to playgroups to pre-schools and childminders, there is a wide range of choices. Choosing the right one for your child will depend on a number of different circumstances, including:

- Convenience to either work or home.
- Your child's personality, and his or her needs.
- Whether the provider accepts any of the payment methods discussed above.
- The cost.
- The hours of opening.

'Finding the right childcare provider for your son or daughter is something you and your partner will want to consider very carefully.'

Finding a nursery

Some primary schools have a nursery department attached to the main school and if the school is likely to be the one you'd prefer your child to attend it would be logical to choose this option if you want your child to attend a day nursery. An advantage of this kind of provider is that using your free nursery entitlement and/or paying for extra provision with childcare vouchers shouldn't be a problem. Disadvantages include the fact that the nursery may only keep school hours, which could cause problems if your own working hours are different, and will almost certainly be closed during school holiday periods.

Private nurseries

Private day-nurseries, by contrast, often offer much longer hours. Many will open at eight o'clock in the morning and continue providing care for children until six o'clock in the evening. For an extra charge some will offer to open even earlier, and they will remain open for all but a few days (typically over the Christmas and Easter periods) each year.

Finding a childminder

As with other childcare and early years' educational providers, childminders must now be registered and inspected. This means that you can obtain a list of the available childminders in your area either by phoning your local Family Information Service (FIS) or online on http://childcarefinder.direct.gov. uk/childcarefinder. But you might want to begin by simply asking other parents, and getting a personal recommendation. Whatever route you take, begin your search as early as possible – good childminders can be difficult to find and the best, of course, will soon fill up.

Sure Start Children's Centres

This government-funded scheme providing free pre-school education has suffered recently from the cuts to public spending, but many areas still operate a service. You can get details from your local authority, although places are limited and you will need to book early. The local Family Information Service (FIS) is another useful source of advice and information regarding Sure Start schemes and providers, and you can get the number of your local FIS by calling 08002 346 346.

All organisations receiving government funding to provide free early education to three- to five-year-olds must by law:

▪ Be included in the relevant Local Authority's Directory of Providers.

▪ Help children in achieving the 'early learning goals' (as set out in the Early Years Foundation Stage).

▪ Be inspected regularly by Ofsted.

All of which is intended to make sure that your child will get a good quality early years' education, regardless of which type of setting they attend.

'Getting the right childcare provider for your son or daughter is something you and your partner will want to consider very carefully. From nursery to playgroups to pre-schools and childminders, there is a wide range of choices.'

Help from your employer

Many employers now offer their employees help to pay for childcare, which can include:

- Paying you cash to pay for childcare.
- Paying the childcare fees directly.
- Paying the child's school fees.

Should you be fortunate enough to have an employer offer any of the above, remember that you will be liable for tax and National Insurance contributions on these payments. There are, however, some types of childcare support provided by employers which are not liable to tax or National Insurance contributions. These include:

- Childcare vouchers.
- Directly contracted childcare.
- Workplace nurseries.

Legal entitlements

There are a range of legal entitlements available for parents, not all of them well known. The gateway for many of these entitlements is having been in employment (with the same employer) for at least a year. If you have, then:

- You have the right to request flexible hours.
- You have the right to request a change to your contracted hours.
- You are entitled to up to thirteen weeks' parental leave per annum (not to be confused with the two weeks' statutory paternity leave).

In addition (and somewhat better known) are the entitlements your partner might qualify for, which include:

- Paid maternity leave.
- Time to attend antenatal appointments.

※ The opportunity to take a full twelve months off work without prejudicing your career.

Maternity leave

As already stated earlier (see chapter 2) your partner will be entitled to take up to 26 weeks of ordinary maternity leave and a further 26 weeks of additional maternity leave. By law, your partner cannot return to work within two weeks of the birth (or four if she works in a factory) whether she wants to or not. This is known as Compulsory Maternity Leave and is the only one of the entitlements about which you don't have a choice.

To qualify for paid maternity leave your partner:

※ Must have been employed (in the same job) continuously for at least 26 weeks before the 15th week before the baby's due date.

※ Must earn an average of at least £95 a week (before tax).

Your entitlement

Your partner is legally entitled to 90% of her average weekly earnings for the first six weeks of her maternity leave. After that she will be paid £123.06 for the remaining 33 weeks that she's entitled to take as paid leave. Some employers offer more generous packages and your partner will need to approach her employer direct to find out if she qualifies for anything other than the statutory paid entitlement. Leave is unpaid from week 39 to 52.

If your partner is unemployed (or self-employed) or hasn't worked for her current employer long enough to qualify for Statutory Maternity Pay she might still be entitled to something called maternity allowance. This is paid at the rate of £123.06 (or 90% of earnings if that figure is lower) and lasts for 39 weeks. To qualify for this your partner must have:

※ Been employed or self-employed for at least 26 of the 66 weeks before the week your baby was due, and

※ Earned an average of £30 over any 13 of those 66 weeks.

Maternity leave Q&A

When can my partner begin her maternity leave?

Your partner can't start her maternity leave until 11 weeks before the baby is due. She needs to give her employer information about when the baby is expected and when she plans to start maternity leave, and the employer must respond to this notification within 28 days.

How much notice does my partner have to give her employer?

At the latest, she needs to have told them both the baby's due date and when she plans to start her maternity leave 15 weeks before the baby is due. Although there is no legal requirement – at this stage – to tell an employer when you plan to return to work, many people will have an idea of when they intend maternity leave to end. But plans change, and your employer is obliged to keep your job open provided you return before the end of your additional maternity leave (the final, unpaid, stretch from weeks 39 to 52).

My partner wants to go in to work for a couple of days during her maternity leave. Is this allowed?

Yes. Your partner can go in for what are known as 'keeping in touch' days up to ten times without affecting her Statutory Maternity Pay.

Returning to work

Legally, your partner's employer is obliged to assume that she will be taking her full 52 weeks maternity leave. Providing them with an earlier return date is merely a courtesy and if she wants to delay her return to work, she can. Having said that, it is clearly important to keep the 'boss' informed. Depending on the nature of the work, they will need to make plans to cover for your partner's absence and it is only fair to give them as much notice as possible if you do intend to change your plans in any way.

Paternity Leave

Since April 2003, fathers and adoptive parents have also had the right to take time off work. Paternity and adoption leave entitlements also apply to partners of the same sex, so although this section refers to 'dads' and 'fathers' it isn't necessarily the case that you have to be a man to access similar rights.

What is paternity leave?

Put bluntly, a fortnight's leave paid at the rate of £123 per week or 90% of your salary if that is lower. Not great, but a start. There is already a move – announced by Nick Clegg in June 2010 – to make parental leave more flexible and give dads a share of the maternity leave entitlement if that's the way a couple want to take it.

As with maternity leave, you have to have been with an employer for a certain period of time before the baby is born, in this case 26 weeks. If you have, then you're entitled to apply for two weeks' paid paternity leave starting from the day on which the baby was born or any other day in the same week. If things don't go to plan, and the birth is either earlier or later than expected, things clearly need to be a little more flexible and you have a 56-day grace period in which to take your paternity leave, should this be the case.

As with maternity leave, you've got to ensure you tell your employer of your plans by the 15th week before the baby is due. You must also either be the child's biological father or the partner/husband of the mother and have (or expect to have) responsibility for the child's upbringing.

'Since April 2003, fathers and adoptive parents have also had the right to take time off work.'

Additional parental leave

This 'new deal for dads' as it was called when it was announced by the government, will apply to those with babies born on or after 3rd April 2011. It allows fathers to take a share of their partner's maternity leave as long as the mother has already taken at least 26 weeks of her entitlement. This could mean, for example, that between them a couple could take an entire year off with their baby, with neither partner being away from work for such a long period of time.

Any outstanding maternity pay will transfer to the father, but remember that from week 39 this stops anyway. Other restrictions include the fact that APL must be taken as one continuous period of leave, must be taken in full week blocks and for a minimum of two weeks.

'The "new deal for dads" will allow dads to take a share of their partner's maternity leave as long as the mother has already taken at least 26 weeks of her entitlement.'

Your rights during and after paternity or additional parental leave

As with maternity leave, a father has the right, following paternity or additional Parental Leave, to return to the same job with the same terms and conditions of employment. You also have the right to request flexible working arrangements to make it easier to cope with the demands of family life.

Rights for adoptive parents

Adoptive parents qualify for a range of similar benefits to natural parents, including the equivalent to maternity leave payments. To qualify for paid adoption leave an employee must:

- Be newly-matched with a child for adoption by an approved adoption agency.
- Have worked continuously for the same employer for 26 weeks up to the week in which they are notified of the match with a adoptive child.

Adoption leave falls into two categories. For the first 26 weeks ordinary adoption leave is granted; this is immediately followed by 26 weeks additional adoption leave making a total of up to 52 weeks. During ordinary and part of additional adoption leave, most adopters will be entitled to Statutory Adoption Pay (SAP) from their employers on a similar basis to SMP (see page 95).

Rights to additional paternity leave and pay when adopting a child apply in essentially the same way as they do following the birth of a child (see page 98).

Statutory adoption pay

SAP is payable for 39 weeks. The rate of SAP is the same as the lower rate of SMP (see page 95). If your average weekly earnings are below the lower earnings limit for National Insurance purposes you won't qualify for SAP but you may qualify for other welfare benefits.

'Adoptive parents qualify for a range of similar benefits to natural parents, including the equivalent of maternity leave payments, allowing them to take time off work when starting family life.'

Summing Up

- Remember, all pregnant women qualify for free NHS dental care and free NHS prescriptions both while they are pregnant and for several months after the birth of their child.

- If either you or your partner are giving up work to look after a child, make sure you receive Child Benefit in your name so that your National Insurance contributions are maintained.

- If you and your partner are earning less than £55,000 per year you may qualify for Child Tax Credit. Contact HM Revenue & Customs and ask for a claim pack. And if your circumstances change (e.g. you get a payrise) don't forget to let HM Revenue & Customs know.

- If you're bringing up a child alone, you can apply for financial help in the form of child maintenance.

- Working parents are entitled to help with the costs of childcare in the form of nursery and childcare vouchers. Make sure you claim what you're entitled to.

- Your local Family Information Service (FIS) can help you find providers of childcare in your area.

Need2Know

Help List

Baby and Father

www.babyandfather.com
A magazine-style website featuring tips and advice as well as up-to-date news on developments relevant to parenting for dads.

Babycentre

www.babycentre.co.uk
Support for parents from pre-conception to birth and beyond.

BBC Parenting

www.bbc.co.uk/parenting
Reliable, authoritative and user-friendly parenting section of the BBC website.

Bringing Up Charlie

www.bringingupcharlie.co.uk
My own award-winning dad's blog. A place to share ideas, swap stories and laugh at my mistakes.

Dads' Space

www.dads-space.com
The site specifically for dads, with information on everything from entertaining the kids to keeping them safe.

Dad Talk

www.dadtalk.co.uk
A place for dads to share information and learn more about being a father.

Department of Health

www.dh.gov.uk/en/index.htm
The Department of Health's website provides policy, guidance and support for health care professionals and members of the public.

Down's Syndrome Association

www.downs-syndrome.org.uk

News, support and information on all matters relating to Down's syndrome.

Families Need Fathers

www.fnf.org.uk

Families Need Fathers provides help and support for parents of either sex concerned with maintaining a relationship with both parents in cases of separation and divorce.

Food Standards Agency

www.eatwell.gov.uk

Advice from the Food Standards Agency about healthy eating as well as up-to-date information about food labelling, allergies and health scares.

FSID

www.fsid.org.uk/

Advice, support and events to help understand, avoid and survive the trauma of Sudden Infant Death.

HM Revenue & Customs

www.hmrc.gov.uk/index.htm

HM Revenue & Customs provides detailed information about tax, allowances and entitlements.

I Can

www.ican.org.uk

For help and advice regarding speech and communication difficulties in children.

Infertility Network UK

www.infertilitynetworkuk.com

The UK's leading infertility support network, providing information for couples having trouble with conception and explaining possible solutions.

National Childbirth Trust

www.nct.org.uk/home
The organisation helping over a million mums and dads each year through pregnancy, childbirth and the early days of parenthood.

National Institute for Clinical Excellence (NICE)

www.nice.org.uk
The National Institute for Clinical Excellence is an independent body providing official guidance on health promotion and the treatment of illness.

Netmums

www.netmums.com
The UK's fastest growing online parenting organisation, with almost 900,000 members. Advice on every aspect of parenting, from finding a playgroup to healthy eating.

Women's Health

www.womens-health.co.uk
Health information and more for your partner.

World Health Organisation (WHO)

www.who.int/en/
The World Health Organisation is the organisation coordinating and directing the health care agenda for the United Nations.

Book List

Further reading

What to Expect in the First Year
Heidi Murkoff (Simon & Schuster Ltd 2010) ISBN: 978-1847379740

What to Expect when you're Expecting
Arlene Eisenberg (Simon & Schuster Ltd; Revised edition 1994)
ISBN: 978-0684817880

The New Contented Little Baby Book
Gina Ford (Vermilion; New edition edition April 2006) ISBN: 978-0091912697

Secrets Of The Baby Whisperer
Tracy Hogg (Vermilion 2001) ISBN: 978-0091857028

Your First Pregnancy – An Essential Guide
Jo Johnson (Need2Know 2009) ISBN: 978-1861440662

The New Father: A Dad's Guide to the First Year
Armin Brott (Mitchell Beazley 2005) ISBN: 978-1845330934

You're Pregnant Too, Mate! The Essential Guide for Expectant Fathers
Gavin Rodgers (Robson Books Ltd1999) ISBN: 978-1861052773

Pregnancy for Men: The Whole Nine Months
Mark Woods (White Ladder Press Ltd 2010) ISBN: 978-190541062

Goodbye, Pert Breasts: The Diary of a Newborn Dad
Ben Wakeling (Lulu 2010) ISBN: 978-1446171349

New Father's Survival Guide
Martyn Cox (Ryland, Peters & Small 2010) ISBN: 978-1845979553

First-Time Parent
Lucy Atkins (Collins 2009) ISBN: 978-0007269440

Pregnancy for Modern Girls: The Naked Truth About Being Pregnant
Hollie Smith (White Ladder Press Ltd 2009) ISBN: 978-1905410606

How to Afford Time Off with your Baby: 101 Ways to Ease the Financial Strain
Becky Goddard-Hill (Vermilion 2009) ISBN: 978-0091924294

Family Friendly Working: Inspiring ideas for making money when you have kids
Antonia Chitty (White Ladder Press Ltd 2008) ISBN: 978-1905410262

The Baby-led Weaning Cookbook
Gill Rapley (Vermilion 2010) ISBN: 978-0091935283

My Daddy Cooks: 100 Fresh New Recipes for the Whole Family
Nick Coffer (Hodder & Stoughton 2011) ISBN: 978-1444713718

Baby's Here! Who Does What?
Duncan Fisher (GS Press 2010) ISBN: 978-1905550050

Infertility - The Essential Guide
Jane Dean (Need2Know) ISBN: 978-1-86144-110-2

Need - 2 - Know

Available Titles Include ...

Allergies A Parent's Guide
ISBN 978-1-86144-064-8 £8.99

Autism A Parent's Guide
ISBN 978-1-86144-069-3 £8.99

Blood Pressure The Essential Guide
ISBN 978-1-86144-067-9 £8.99

Dyslexia and Other Learning Difficulties
A Parent's Guide ISBN 978-1-86144-042-6 £8.99

Bullying A Parent's Guide
ISBN 978-1-86144-044-0 £8.99

Epilepsy The Essential Guide
ISBN 978-1-86144-063-1 £8.99

Your First Pregnancy The Essential Guide
ISBN 978-1-86144-066-2 £8.99

Gap Years The Essential Guide
ISBN 978-1-86144-079-2 £8.99

Secondary School A Parent's Guide
ISBN 978-1-86144-093-8 £9.99

Primary School A Parent's Guide
ISBN 978-1-86144-088-4 £9.99

Applying to University The Essential Guide
ISBN 978-1-86144-052-5 £8.99

ADHD The Essential Guide
ISBN 978-1-86144-060-0 £8.99

Student Cookbook – Healthy Eating The Essential Guide
ISBN 978-1-86144-069-3 £8.99

Multiple Sclerosis The Essential Guide
ISBN 978-1-86144-086-0 £8.99

Coeliac Disease The Essential Guide
ISBN 978-1-86144-087-7 £9.99

Special Educational Needs A Parent's Guide
ISBN 978-1-86144-116-4 £9.99

The Pill An Essential Guide
ISBN 978-1-86144-058-7 £8.99

University A Survival Guide
ISBN 978-1-86144-072-3 £8.99

View the full range at **www.need2knowbooks.co.uk**.
To order our titles call **01733 898103**, email **sales@ n2kbooks.com** or visit the website. Selected ebooks available online.

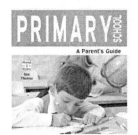

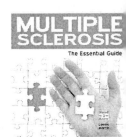

Need - 2 - Know, Remus House, Coltsfoot Drive, Peterborough, PE2 9BF